"After years of trusting her as our book wh... finally written a book for us! This is the book I didn't even know I was waiting for. I can't wait to share it with everyone I know."

—**Emily P. Freeman,** *Wall Street Journal* bestselling author of *Simply Tuesday*

"Anne Bogel is a smart, savvy, kindhearted woman of wisdom whose words continually have me nodding my head in agreement and saying, 'I thought *I* was the only one!' This book, and all of her future books, will have a prominent space on my shelf. The world is better because of her insight."

—**Tsh Oxenreider,** author of *At Home in the World* and *Notes from a Blue Bike*

"As someone who loves analyzing myself, my family, and my friends and learning more about what makes each of us unique, I absolutely adored *Reading People*. This book hasn't just impacted me as a parent. Understanding more about how people are wired through the research, data, and examples Anne gives is helping me in every relationship. Truly, I feel like I'm a better wife, mom, employer, friend, and person for having read this book."

—**Crystal Paine,** *New York Times* bestselling author of *Say Goodbye to Survival Mode* and founder of MoneySavingMom.com

"You possibly picked up this book because you want to understand someone around you who might be, how should I say this, difficult. This book will most certainly help you understand them better, but what I suspect might happen along the way is that you will begin to understand *yourself* better. Anne lays out so many different ways to view and understand our own personalities, as well as those around us. This book will help you be a better parent, spouse, friend, boss, employee, and more. Personal relationships are core to our existence, and this book in your hands will help your relationships go deeper and last longer because of the greater understanding you will have for yourself and those around you."

—**Jamie Ivey,** author and host of *The Happy Hour* podcast

CALGARY PUBLIC LIBRARY

JAN   2018

"For years I've been seeking out Anne's impeccable advice on what books to read, and at first glance I thought this book was all about the people who read—and it is. Surprise! Books aren't the only thing we can read. *Reading People* is the perfect reminder that the most important reading assignment you'll ever have might be sitting at the dinner table with you and staring back at you in the mirror."

—**Myquillyn Smith**, author of *The Nesting Place*

"Whether you're an Enneagram guru, a Myers-Briggs Type Indicator nerd, a StrengthsFinder coach, or a personality-test novice, you'll find something in *Reading People*. In these pages, Anne examines the personality tests that measure our individuality, but more importantly, she uses those tests to highlight a beautiful truth: our personalities are what make us utterly unique, perfectly human, and ultimately beautiful."

—**Seth Haines**, author of *Coming Clean*

"*Reading People* is a game-changing book. It empowers us to see both ourselves and others in a more gracious manner and offers useful ideas for how to build stronger and healthier relationships. The wisdom Anne Bogel packs in *Reading People* is insightful, easy-to-understand, and life-giving."

—**Jessica N. Turner**, author of *The Fringe Hours*

"Anne Bogel delivers a fantastically useful and practical guide to personality frameworks that cuts through the hype, false promises, and personality parlor tricks. This is a concise, highly readable guide to the Enneagram, the Myers-Briggs Type Indicator, and other personality tools that draws deeply from stories of her own growth and extensive reading."

—**Ed Cyzewski**, author of *A Christian Survival Guide* and *Coffeehouse Theology*

Reading People

Reading People

how seeing the world through the
lens of personality changes everything

Anne Bogel

BakerBooks

a division of Baker Publishing Group
Grand Rapids, Michigan

© 2017 by Anne Bogel

Published by Baker Books
a division of Baker Publishing Group
P.O. Box 6287, Grand Rapids, MI 49516-6287
www.bakerbooks.com

Printed in the United States of America

All rights reserved. No part of this publication may be reproduced, stored in a retrieval system, or transmitted in any form or by any means—for example, electronic, photocopy, recording—without the prior written permission of the publisher. The only exception is brief quotations in printed reviews.

Library of Congress Cataloging-in-Publication Data
Names: Bogel, Anne, 1978– author.
Title: Reading people : how seeing the world through the lens of personality changes everything / Anne Bogel.
Description: Grand Rapids, MI : Baker Books, a division of Baker Publishing Group, [2017] | Includes bibliographical references.
Identifiers: LCCN 2017015996 | ISBN 9780801072918 (pbk.)
Subjects: LCSH: Myers-Briggs Type Indicator. | Typology (Psychology) | Personality.
Classification: LCC BF698.8.M94 B64 2017 | DDC 155.2—dc23
LC record available at https://lccn.loc.gov/2017015996

Unless otherwise indicated, Scripture quotations are from the Holy Bible, New International Version®. NIV®. Copyright © 1973, 1978, 1984, 2011 by Biblica, Inc.™ Used by permission of Zondervan. All rights reserved worldwide. www.zondervan.com

Scripture quotations labeled KJV are from the King James Version of the Bible.

Myers-Briggs Type Indicator, Myers-Briggs, MBTI, and MBTI Logo are trademarks or registered trademarks of the MBTI® Trust, Inc., in the United States and other countries.

The author is represented by the William K. Jensen Literary Agency.

17 18 19 20 21 22 23   8 7 6 5 4

In keeping with biblical principles of creation stewardship, Baker Publishing Group advocates the responsible use of our natural resources. As a member of the Green Press Initiative, our company uses recycled paper when possible. The text paper of this book is composed in part of post-consumer waste.

For Will,
who gets me

Contents

Introduction

a noble pursuit

The BuzzFeed-style quiz is taking over the internet, serving up answers to questions no one is asking. What *Star Wars* character are you? What restaurant trend describes your personality? Which Hogwarts house suits you best? What city should you actually live in? Which Ryan Gosling character is your soul mate? What's your superpower? Your work style?

These addictive quizzes make it easy to put ourselves in (very weird) boxes. And if my Facebook feed is any indication, people can't resist taking these quizzes and sharing their results—no matter how inane the topic or how small the insight offered. Underpinning these quizzes is the core assumption that we won't have the same answers. We are all different—in matters both serious and silly—and discovering those differences is strangely enjoyable. Cynics argue that we're drawn to these simple check-the-box quizzes because we're ill-equipped to deal with the complexity of real life, but I believe this trend points to something more substantial.

We're not just looking for a way to kill five minutes online. Our methods may be questionable, but our motives are pure: we truly want to know more about ourselves and the people we interact with every day. We suspect our lives would be better if we actually understood ourselves and the people we love. We want to know why we do what we do, think what we think, act how we act—and why *they* do too.

But what we're finding is this: *actually knowing ourselves* isn't as easy as taking a few check-the-box quizzes on the internet. We're surprised to discover that it's difficult to perceive ourselves for who we really are. That information would be infinitely more useful, but it's also harder to come by. Since we don't know where to start to find the good stuff—the genuinely helpful information about ourselves and the people we love—we settle for discovering which defunct '90s soda we are or which Jane Austen leading man we're meant to marry. But if we instead knew the right questions to ask ourselves—the ones that would give us true insight into our inner selves—and approached those questions with the same playful spirit (and perhaps just a smidge more seriousness and self-reflection), we could emerge with life-changing information. We could learn to read people better—ourselves and others.

What Makes You *You*

This struggle to define ourselves isn't some narcissistic fad driven by social media. Our collective fascination with understanding ourselves—and, specifically, understanding our personalities— goes back much further than that, to way before the days of the internet. We've known for a long time that we don't begin our lives as identical blank slates. For thousands of years, writers, philosophers, and even biblical heroes have teased out the differences in human nature. We can find personality references in the writings of Socrates and Shakespeare, as well as in the writings of the desert fathers and America's founding fathers. When Paul wrote to the Corinthians, "There are different kinds of gifts, but the same Spirit distributes them" (1 Corinthians 12:4), I imagine he was speaking not only of spiritual gifts but also of personality traits. (Paul himself was certainly known for *his* fiery personality and was under no illusions few were quite like him.)

When we talk about someone's personality, we're referring to those characteristic patterns of thoughts, feelings, and behaviors that make that person unique. We're all inclined to think, feel, and act in particular ways. Our personalities capture what we're likely to find relaxing or exciting or pleasurable or tough. This core set of qualities is a huge part of what makes you *you*.

Current research indicates that personality traits are hardwired; they're largely hereditary and remain relatively constant throughout our lives.[1] If we're outgoing or reserved, energetic or subdued, we deserve neither credit nor blame for those traits. We just came that way, out of the box, and we can't trade ourselves in for a different model.

While personality is a key part of who you are, it's just one of many things that make you *you*. Many important traits don't fall under the personality umbrella. Kindness, generosity, honesty, patience—these are all examples of character traits that interact with but are distinct from personality. It's easy to conflate character with personality; it's a common mistake. We've all met someone charming but dastardly, if not in the neighborhood then in a favorite novel.

And we all act "out of character" sometimes. Our behaviors fluctuate with our moods and our circumstances. People behave differently when they can see themselves in a mirror, for instance. But our behavior fluctuates in predictable ways. Everyone does certain things at certain times (such as wanting to be alone), but some people want to be alone a heck of a lot more than others.

Compared to our personality traits, character traits are more malleable. Our personalities can only be managed (or tamed, some might say). Our characters *can* be shaped, although this isn't easy and happens slowly, with effort. Much of what we call character arises out of our core beliefs, and it's surprisingly difficult to change our beliefs.

In addition to our character traits, we all have unique skills, abilities, and passions. We have personal experiences, histories, and hang-ups that shape us. These also interact with our personalities, and the way they impact us may even depend on our personalities, but they are not the same thing as our personalities.

We are complex and fascinating beings. These various aspects of ourselves—our personalities, our characters, our skills, the essence that truly makes us who we are—combine in an infinite variety of ways to make each of us who we are.

Like Holding a Good Map

Changing our core personality traits is difficult, if not impossible. To a large extent, personality is something we must learn to live with—whether that means accepting our own personalities or that of a spouse, parent, child, boss, friend, or neighbor. A big part of learning about personality is learning to make peace with who we are. But if we use personality insights well, we wouldn't dream of stopping there.

14

The more I've learned about personality, the more I've discovered how powerful this knowledge can be. The various personality frameworks presented in this book are incredible tools for understanding why we do the things we do, why some things come easy while others are difficult, why particular things about our dearest friends drive us crazy, or why we absolutely cannot stand to watch network news or listen to rap music or make small talk without sounding like a blubbering idiot. And personality insights allow us to understand why other people do the things *they* do, even when (especially when) their thoughts, feelings, and actions in a given situation are profoundly different from our own.

Prior to us understanding more about personality, their behavior may have baffled us. We can't fathom why a loved one hides when the doorbell rings or a coworker must understand the origin of every single *Hamilton* lyric or a friend genuinely enjoys chatting with the customer service representative on the other end of the phone line. They're not crazy; they're just not *us*. They are hardwired differently than we are, and personality insights explain why and how.

I've come to think understanding personality is like holding a good map. That map can't take you anywhere. It doesn't change your location; you're still right where you were before. But the map's purpose isn't to move you; it's to show you the lay of the land. It's the tool that makes it possible for you to get where you want to go.

Practical and Actionable

In recent years, I've learned to accept and adapt my behavior for my personality type—and for the types of those around me—in ways that never would have occurred to me ten, or even two, years ago. I've leaned heavily on personality insights to help me

- structure my days in a way that helps me not only survive but also thrive;
- recognize when I'm feeling out of sorts and how to best deal with those feelings;
- not lose my cool (or my mojo) over the marathon week of family Christmas gatherings;
- understand why action movies and horror novels are too much for me;
- realize I wasn't necessarily a terrible Christian, just an introverted Christian in an extroverted church;
- plan my day so I don't hit a wall at 4:00 p.m. every afternoon; and
- identify what my dream job might look like and stay away from jobs that would be soul-sucking for me.

Additionally, I've gained meaningful insights into other people from studying personality. These takeaways have changed the way I interact with them and have helped me figure out

- why some of my girlfriends prefer margarita night for ten, while others prefer coffee for two or three;
- how to stop the terrible conflict cycle my husband and I were locked in;
- how not to lose my mind (well, most days) during the pre-dinner hour at my house with my loud and crazy family of six;
- how to choose the right church for my family; and

• how to tell the difference between when my kid is being quirky and when I have a real problem that needs outside help.

These are just a few of the concrete, practical changes I've made in my life thanks to understanding the personality frameworks I highlight in this book. This knowledge didn't require a great deal of study or a huge time investment. To understand the frameworks and what they told me about my personality, as well as the personalities of the people I interact with every day, I needed to ask the right questions of myself and pay attention to some specific moments in life.

The Insight that Changes Everything

Have you ever seen the movie *The Sixth Sense*? Okay, I've actually seen only a few clips, not the whole movie, because I'm a highly sensitive person (HSP) and M. Night Shyamalan freaks me out. (We'll talk about HSPs in chapter 3.) But the movie has so permeated popular culture that even people who haven't seen it know about the twist ending.

This supernatural thriller is about the relationship between a little boy named Cole Sear (played by Haley Joel Osment) and Dr. Malcolm Crowe (played by Bruce Willis), the psychiatrist enlisted to help him. Cole has a secret ability to communicate with dead people. As Dr. Crowe teaches Cole to release the ghosts that scare him by offering them help, he learns that maybe he wasn't summoned to help Cole. Perhaps it's the other way around.

In a surprise ending, we discover that Crowe has been dead from the beginning. It explains why his wife won't talk to him, why she doesn't even acknowledge his existence. For two hours, viewers are led to believe that she is ignoring him because their marriage is awful, but it turns out she can't even see him. With the big reveal, our minds reel as we mentally flip back through the movie to incorporate this key piece of information into our understanding, which casts the film's events in a whole new light. Once we know Crowe is dead, the narrative shifts and everything makes perfect sense. We think, *Oh, of course,* even though while we were watching the movie the first time, we never perceived anything was amiss.

Try this for a more relatable example. Have you ever had a really bad day? A day when nothing seemed to be going your way and you were tired and moody and agitated and nobody liked you and you didn't like them either and you couldn't put your finger on what was going so terribly wrong? Then you ate a sandwich (or, better yet, took a nap) and felt like a brand-new person, and you realized that nothing was horribly amiss, you were just hangry. Or maybe slangry. (You can figure out what *that* means, right?)[2]

That little insight completely reframed the way you felt about the previous few hours.

If you're a parent, you're acquainted with the phenomenon when your two-year-old is having a really terrible afternoon and won't eat their snack and won't keep their clothes on and won't say anything but no and screams for no reason and you fear that you're a terrible parent who has ruined *everything,* until your child finally wears themselves out and collapses on the sofa, snoring, three hours before bedtime, and you realize, *My child isn't possessed; they were just exhausted.*

Personality insights can be like this. One key piece of information shifts our whole paradigm—and the world suddenly makes a lot more sense.

The frameworks in this book can highlight what upsets you (and why) and what makes you hum. They can help you understand what's causing friction in your relationships, and what to do about it. They can open your eyes to what's *really* going on in situations that currently make you batty.

Unfortunately, finding this information about our own personalities isn't a straightforward process. It's not exactly complicated; it's just that it's difficult to look directly at our own natures. That's why I rely on the tool of personality frameworks. These frameworks give us the eyes we need to see ourselves in a new way.

Seeing the World through Someone Else's Eyes

I'm a big reader. In fact, I have a blog called *Modern Mrs. Darcy* (modernmrsdarcy.com), where I share what I'm reading, recommend books to others, or—my favorite—connect what I read in a book to the real, off-the-page life I'm living.

I read a wide variety of books, across many genres, but what I *really* love is to crack open a good novel and step into another world for three hundred pages. When I read a great story, I get to experience the world through someone else's eyes for a little while. I'll never be a boy wizard, but J. K. Rowling helps me imagine what it might be like to be a kid shouldering a fearsome responsibility (while wielding my wand and chugging butter beer). I live in the twenty-first century, but Jane Austen helps me feel the pleasures and perils of life in the English countryside two hundred years ago. I had a wonderful childhood, and my parents are still alive and well, living just a few miles down the road, but L. M. Montgomery invites me to experience the sting of being told I'm unwanted, the loneliness of having no one to love or care for me.

I love the personality frameworks in this book because they let me do the same thing.

We all live in the first person. I experience the world through *my* eyes; we all do. But each of these personality frameworks, when used thoughtfully, gives me eyes to see the world from someone else's point of view for a little while. It's a simple way to try out a new perspective, a different worldview. And once we've caught a glimpse of the world through someone else's eyes, we won't soon forget that point of view. It changes us, and it changes the way we read others.

About This Book

I've shared some of my personality-related stories on my blog over the years, and as I've interacted with readers, I've gotten to hear just how helpful learning about personality has been for many of them. But a big obstacle for many people who would like to learn more about these frameworks is the sheer amount of information out there. It's overwhelming. People don't know where to begin or which framework will help them most or where to find the best resources or why to even bother.

My goal in this book is threefold. In these pages, I hope to

1. provide an overview of the frameworks that have been the most helpful to me;
2. make this important information a lot more accessible and a lot less intimidating; and
3. highlight the kind of valuable insights that come from understanding personality.

Keep in mind that I'm not a scholar. I'm a fellow traveler, someone who has benefited from the same information and has learned to pay attention to the right moments, ask the right questions of myself, and tweak accordingly. I'll hold your hand and show you how I've been able to put what I've learned to use in my own life in an effort to inspire and guide you to do the same.

You don't have to read this book straight through from front to back. In fact, I'd suggest you *don't*. After reading about my *aha!* moment in chapter 1, feel free to jump to the framework that interests you most. I haven't shared every existing personality framework in this book but instead have chosen the ones that have helped me most. Now, *you* get to choose the ones that look helpful to you. Read a few chapters, take an assessment or two, talk it all over with a friend, and come back to the book when you're ready. Some frameworks are easier to grasp than others. Some make intuitive sense after your first read, while others may require a reread for them to really sink in. (I'm looking at you, chapter 7.) This book will wait for you.

You don't have to be an expert about personality to enjoy the benefits of this book, but you do need to cultivate an expertise about yourself. I promise, it's nobler than it sounds. I'll be right here, asking the questions right along with you.

1

My Aha! Moment

understanding my personality type

I've been fascinated with personality since one memorable family dinner when I was in my late tweens or early teens. My mom mentioned her church group would be reading a new book together. I'd never heard of the book and didn't know much about the subject matter, but what my mom said intrigued me.

She explained that the author had taken an old idea and updated it for the twentieth century. Ancient Greek and Roman physicians and philosophers had sorted people into four categories based on their "humors," believing each individual's unique combination of these elements determined their personality. For the modernized version, the four categories of people are the popular sanguine, powerful choleric, perfect melancholy, and peaceful phlegmatic. These categories aren't good or bad. There is no "right" answer, only the possibility to accurately see yourself as you truly are. The promise is that when you understand yourself better—your strengths and weaknesses, emotional needs, and driving motivations—it is much easier to understand others as well, especially when they aren't like you.

I begged my mom to share her copy of the book and spent hours and hours poring over it, trying to spot myself and my loved ones in its pages. I was hooked.[1]

I became obsessed with the idea that by discovering who I was at my core—what made me tick, who God made me to be—I could gain insight into important questions, such as What should I study? Who should I marry? What do I want to be when I grow up? How am I going to remember to buy milk at the grocery store?

I surmised that finding the right answers to these questions—the profound and the prosaic—would change my life.

But they didn't—or not for a long time, at least. That's because even though I was fascinated by personality typing and started learning more about it, I was doing it all wrong. When it came to connecting what I was learning to my real life, I was failing. Totally.

Wait a minute, you say. I thought that with personality there *are* no wrong answers?

Well, yes and no.

Objectively speaking, when it comes to your personality type—at least according to the frameworks in this book—there are no wrong answers. No personality type is better or worse than any other. Some people are better suited than others to be engineers or teachers or executives, while others are naturally more compassionate or more analytical. It takes all kinds to make a world.[2]

But there is a wrong way to *approach* personality, and I had inadvertently found it.

An Inadvertent but Common Error

When I initially tried to figure out my personality, the crucial first step in understanding myself and others, I didn't begin at the beginning. I didn't ask myself what I was really like. Instead, I asked myself what I *wished* I were like.

It was an inadvertent error, and so insidious I didn't even realize I was doing it. (And I wasn't alone. When it comes to personality frameworks, this happens *all the time*.) But my understandable mistake still ruined my chances of gaining any useful self-knowledge from the experience.

To illustrate, let me tell you how much I hate parking garages. It relates, I promise.

When it comes to operating a large motor vehicle—and by large, I mean "bigger than a bicycle"—my spatial abilities are, er, not great. This isn't a big deal (my driving record is beautiful, honestly), unless I'm parking. Parking is hard. I can manage just fine in a suburban parking lot or my own driveway (don't laugh). But put me in a parking garage, and I start shaking.

I don't know about the parking garages in your town, but in the garage I regularly have the displeasure of parking in, it's important that I pull my car *all the way in* to the parking space or my Honda's back end (did you notice how I avoided saying "minivan"?) will block the driving lane. In theory, this is no big deal. But in practice, this means cringing with every fiber of my being as I ease the front end of my vehicle closer and closer to an immovable concrete wall—inch by uncomfortable inch—dreading the repugnant metal-on-concrete scraping noise (and costly-to-repair damage) that will result if I misjudge the distance.

When I first started parking in this awful garage, I would pull my car in just as close as I could bear. Then I'd kill the

25

engine, hop out, check out my parking job, and discover I was still a full two feet from the barricade. I wish I were kidding.

My early experience with personality frameworks was a lot like parking in that garage.

I remember in college when I first really dove into the Myers-Briggs Type Indicator (MBTI)®. The system identifies and describes sixteen distinct personalities, which we'll learn more about in chapter 6, but for now, suffice it to say, it's important to *accurately* identify your type. I spent hours poring over the various profiles and found the information simultaneously fascinating and frustrating.

When I first took the assessment, my result was clear: INTJ. For those of you to whom this sounds like total alphabet soup, allow me to explain. The INTJ is known as the architect, the mastermind, the scientist. This result was no surprise, given my history and upbringing; many INTJs are little bookworms as kids. They're smart and creative and highly analytical. They prefer to work alone or, at the very most, in small groups. These types are hardworking and determined; they think critically and clearly; they tend to be perfectionists. They grow up to become software and mechanical engineers, project managers, marketing analysts, and attorneys.

I knew the INTJ type, all right. I come from a long line of attorneys and judges and knew the type and their skills very well, even if I hadn't known to put the alphabet soup label on it. Those skills were valued in my household growing up. Perhaps that's why it was so easy for me to see myself as an INTJ. And because I knew the type so well, I didn't realize a critical flaw in my thinking. I didn't see the INTJ type as *one* way to be; I thought it was *the* way to be. So I wasn't surprised when my personality test confirmed that I was a rationalist type who could grow up to become a terrific attorney one day.

In my assumptions, I completely misunderstood myself, yet I had no clue I had done this. Instead, I continued merrily on my way, convinced I was a strategic thinker and analytical planner and occasionally wondering why this "insight" didn't seem to help me much in my day-to-day life. I thought my parking job was just fine.

I was wrong. I was still three feet from the barrier, and my back end was blocking the lane.

I spent hours studying the various MBTI profiles, again fascinated and frustrated. And again, I had new information but no insight.

I wasn't looking for knowledge for knowledge's sake. I wanted practical information I could put into action. I wanted to cash in on the promise of the first personality book that hooked me: that I could understand others better by first understanding myself better. Unfortunately, the information wasn't helpful to me because, while I was gaining an understanding of personality typing systems in general, I still didn't understand what I was really like. I didn't have a correct understanding of my own personality.

Thales of Miletus, one of the sages of ancient Greece, put it plainly: "The most difficult thing in life is to know yourself."[3] Without realizing it, I had bumped straight into a key problem the Greeks identified more than two thousand years ago: knowing yourself may sound easy, but it's surprisingly complicated. I was just a kid; I had no deep-seated, long-established wisdom. I had a lot to learn about myself, and I was just getting started.

Looking back, I wonder, *How could I have gotten myself so wrong? How could I have misunderstood myself so thoroughly?*

Perhaps, because I was young, I didn't have the life experience I needed to see a person clearly, even if that person was me. However, I place the bulk of the blame on my own blindness, caused by plain old wishful thinking.

Denial Is a Powerful Force

I have an obstetrician friend who has delivered thousands of babies, including a surprisingly high number from women who didn't know they were pregnant. Having carried four babies to term, this blows my mind. I'd expect one such delivery over the course of a career, *maybe*. But my doctor friend has seen dozens—and he's still young. When he first told me this, I thought he was making it up just to get a laugh, but he was being truthful. When I asked how this could possibly happen over and over again, he explained that, in all seriousness, denial is a powerful force. Or as Christopher Alexander said, "We are not always comfortable with the true self that lies deep within us."[4]

Whether my own mistake—of seeing only what I *wanted* to see—was born of ignorance or deep-rooted discomfort, I know this much: when it comes to understanding yourself and others, wishful thinking will get you nowhere. If personality information is going to help you, you're going to have to get comfortable with the true self that lies deep within you.

All the personality tests in the world won't mean anything to you if you're not honest with yourself about your own personality and the personalities of those around you. Aspirational answers won't do you any good; only true ones will. And so, the first step is to take an unflinching look at who you truly are. What are you *really* like?

The Beginning of Understanding

Fast-forward a few years to the winter following my June wedding. My husband, Will, and I had just had another painful fight. It was awful, but not in the way you'd imagine. We hadn't fought about anything earth-shaking. Our conflicts were excruciating because we lacked the skills we needed to work through routine marital disagreements.

It doesn't matter how often couples fight. However, *how* they fight is critical. Married people need to learn how to disagree, figure things out, and move on. Will and I were married, but we hadn't figured out how to do those things yet. That first winter we were still terrible at conflict. When we disagreed, he became cold and distant. I was extraordinarily sensitive to his change of mood, and I'd get upset, which baffled him. Then I'd become angry because he didn't understand why I was upset. Secretly (or maybe not so secretly), I thought I was being reasonable and Will was doing it wrong. I blamed him for shutting down whenever we disagreed, and I told him so. Often.

Back to the fight. I don't remember what it was about—how to fold the laundry, where to store the Tupperware, what we should do on Saturday morning—whatever it was, it was mind-numbingly mundane. But we disagreed, as people do. Then I told Will what I thought, and he acted aloof, then I got upset, and then he was baffled—which made me furious!

Instead of talking circles around our stupid issue again, I did the only thing that seemed to help—I went for a run in the freezing cold to cool off. Then I came home, took a shower, put on my pajamas, and plopped on the couch with a library book. Coincidentally, I was reading David Keirsey's *Please Understand Me II*, which I now jokingly call the MBTI Bible.

The previous year Will and I had gone through our church's required premarital counseling program. We drove across town on a Saturday afternoon to meet the couple we'd been randomly paired with. They were kind, if a bit eccentric. I can still remember our surprise when we pulled into their driveway and saw three hundred pairs of teddy bear eyes staring at us from their home's bay window.

We drank lukewarm tea and made awkward chitchat at their kitchen table under the watchful eyes of the teddy bears, which lined not just the bay window but every room of the home. After the introductions were over, they presented us each with a personality assessment and a number 2 pencil. Our future discussions would be based on our results.

We spent the next half hour bubbling in answers to a few hundred questions about how we handle conflict, what we dream of, how often we seek out new experiences, and if we tend to be agreeable. A month later, we returned to the land of the teddy bears to find out how we did.

According to our results, we were more or less compatible, more alike than different. "There's one thing we noticed," our hosts said. "Your tests indicate that you might have problems with conflict. But don't worry too much. All couples do."

I found the whole experience frustrating. What kind of conflict—and why? What would we do about it when it happened? I felt as though I'd spent too much time bubbling in answers to get a result that felt like the kind of "wisdom" I could find in a fortune cookie.

I was dissatisfied because, again, I was so close to discovering some genuinely useful information. Could Will and I truly use some good info about our strengths and weaknesses, sticking points, and blind spots? You betcha. We didn't get it there, but when we left that day, I felt as though it was possible to find that kind of information *somewhere*.

Like the book nerd I was, I took myself to my friendly local library and started looking for books about personality types. (This was in the days of dial-up internet, so I consulted my local library, not Google. A good thing, I think.) I came home that night with a long reading list.

Because of the typical pre-wedding craziness, I didn't start reading those books until *after* the wedding. Trust me on this: spending the first winter of your married life reading books about personality isn't a terrible way to begin.

Most of what I read went straight over my head, but I was learning. I wasn't yet able to see myself clearly in any of the profiles. I still felt clueless about my inner workings, my strengths and weaknesses. But I was at least acutely sensitive to the fact that everyone innately has strengths *and* weaknesses and that all people are different—*very* different—and that isn't a bad thing.

I couldn't type myself, but I was beginning to suspect I'd been all wrong about the INTJ diagnosis. I was studying up, trying to find myself (for real this time) in the type descriptions.

So I sat at home on my couch, in my comfy pajamas, with a copy of *Please Understand Me II* from the library and a hot cup of tea. I flipped it open and started reading.

It Changes Nothing; It Changes Everything

That night I opened my book to a new chapter in *Please Understand Me II*, where I'd left off the night before. That chapter was all about temperament and romantic relationships, including the strengths and weaknesses for different pairings in married life. When I came to the part where David Keirsey explains how the Rational (NT) types function in married life, and especially what a pairing between the Rational and the Idealist (NF) looks like, my jaw fell open. *That was us.* He was describing Will (clearly an NT) and me (who must be an NF) so accurately it was spooky. It was as though I was reading the history of my courtship and early marriage, right there on the page. (Don't worry about the alphabet soup. We'll get there.)

Here's what I learned that night. First, because of Keirsey's dead-on description of the way an Idealist tends to handle conflict unhealthily, I was absolutely sure I'd been typing myself incorrectly. (This would be the first of many times I would discover that the easiest way to type yourself is to pay attention to how you're likely to screw up.) For the first time, I could see clearly that my behavior matched the NF type. The description was so uncannily accurate in regard to my behavior that I knew *instantly* I'd been typing myself incorrectly for years. It was suddenly clear where I'd gone wrong: I hadn't been seeing myself as I actually was but as I wanted to be. No wonder those personality rubrics hadn't helped me.

Contrary to my belief, Will, who I could now clearly peg as an NT, wasn't terrible at conflict. In fact, his approach to marital disagreements was textbook for his MBTI type. And my behavior was textbook for mine. We were experiencing what Keirsey called "an endless problem"[5] in relationships between our types (which, except for this sticking point, Keirsey declares are extremely well-suited for marriage). My type is naturally emotionally expressive; Will's type is naturally resistant to emotional displays. When we disagreed, I would tell Will how I felt, and he would remain calm, seemingly cold. I thought that meant he didn't understand me, or care, and I'd get upset. He didn't understand why I was upset, because he definitely understood—and felt my disappointment deeply. Then I'd get angry that he seemed not to understand.

That night I finally understood that Will wasn't being cold or trying to exasperate me. He just wasn't *me*, and I'd been expecting him to act like me.

I cannot tell you how freeing this insight was. Let's just say the clouds parted and I'm pretty sure the angels sang. We were still the people we'd been the day before, a couple who still didn't know how to fight. But that discovery dialed our conflicts down from *epic* to *ordinary*. Our disagreements weren't alarming; they were normal. Expected, even. My epiphany didn't change anything except our perspective—not that day, at least—but it changed the way I moved forward.

For the first time, I began to see the dynamics at play when Will and I disagreed in a new light. It was my first big *aha!* moment about personality, the first time I felt the power of having accurate information about my personality (and, in this case, my husband's personality) and applying it to my life. Once I understood what was actually going on, and why, I could begin to do something about it.

Maybe when I first started exploring personality—and couldn't get mine right—I'd made an honest mistake. Maybe I simply wasn't comfortable with the true self that lay deep within me. But I suspect the problem was simply this: knowing yourself is *hard*. It's difficult to clearly see yourself for who you really are. The process requires that you ask a difficult question of yourself and face the answer with as much honesty and grace as you can muster, because sometimes "What am I really like?" is a scary question.

Asking yourself this question and facing the answer is intense, but it's also possible—and absolutely worth it.

Probing your own personality isn't an easy process, not even in the best scenario. But I'm keenly aware of how my frustrating experience could have been *so much easier* if I'd known—even a little bit—what I was doing. Looking back, I wish someone had pointed me in the right direction. I wish I'd had someone looking over my shoulder, encouraging me when I headed in the right direction, and gently calling me back when I wandered off track. I needed someone to ask me the right questions at the right moments and to point out the key things I should have been paying attention to. I'm a big reader, so I wouldn't have minded if this guidance had existed in the pages of a good book. I can't go back and smooth my own road, but maybe my experience can make yours a little less bumpy. Stay with me, as that's what I hope to do in the chapters ahead.

2

Communication Breakdown

introverts and extroverts

"Anne, this is my friend Mrs. Baker."

"*Anne*, this is my friend *Mrs. Baker.*"

"ANNE, this is my friend MRS. BAKER."

My mom was trying to get me to say, "Hello, Mrs. Baker, how are you?" but my six-year-old self just couldn't do it. First, I was introverted and hated talking to strangers (and a good many nonstrangers). Second, I thought that was a dumb thing for a kid to say. I didn't know any other six-year-olds who talked like that.

I was a good girl, the kind who never got in trouble—except for in moments like these.

My mother didn't understand my reserve, and we battled over these sorts of introductions for years. In hindsight, our dynamic makes sense. My mom is an extrovert to the core, a vivacious people person, the sort who's never met a stranger. She loves being out in the world; she's always loved meeting new people and making new connections. She revels in introducing her husband, friend, or daughter to her third-grade teacher's mother's next-door neighbor. Or her best friend's little brother's mail carrier.

"What a delightful small world it is!" she'd often say to me.

Mom couldn't imagine that not everyone thought it was a delight and a joy to chatter for hours about anything at all with friends, acquaintances, and strangers and that I wouldn't likewise enjoy meeting them and learning all about their personal histories. It never occurred to her that her introverted daughter didn't enjoy being constantly on the go, meeting new people and connecting with old ones.

My mom thought I was being cheeky, tapping into my latent rebellious side. She was baffled by the outright refusal of her otherwise obedient daughter to cooperate on this one point. She didn't understand until many years later that I was an introverted kid, reacting exactly as you'd expect an introvert of any age to react when forced into such a situation. It was as though I was right-handed and she was asking me to write with my left. I couldn't do it. Nor did I want to.

What You Need to Know about Introverts and Extroverts

What both my mom and I know now that we didn't understand then is that introverts and extroverts are prone to misunderstanding one another. Introverts are often thought to be shy, and they may battle the perception that they dislike people or company or that they're grouchy or social misfits. Extroverts, however, battle the perception that they're flighty or shallow or relentlessly happy. People tend to assume extroverts are bad listeners, hate being alone, and are irrationally "needy" for the company of others.

To truly understand introversion and extroversion, we need to cut through the misconceptions and grasp what these terms really mean.

Grammar geek alert: *introvert* and *extrovert* are verbs as well as nouns (although, to get even geekier, the verb form is actually *extravert*). And to further complicate matters, Carl Jung spelled *his* noun "extravert," but the modern spelling is more often "extrovert." You will see the words spelled both ways throughout this book, depending on the context.

The North and South of Temperament

Even though Carl Jung first introduced the terms *introvert* and *extravert* back in 1921 (in his now-classic volume *Psychological Types*), the concepts—especially introversion—crashed into the public's consciousness in 2012 with the publication of Susan Cain's *Quiet*, which greatly increased awareness of "the power of introverts in a world that can't stop talking."[1]

Cain succinctly defines introverts as "people who prefer quieter, more minimally stimulating environments," compared to extroverts, who seek out—and even thrive on—noise and stimulation.[2] Introverts are fundamentally attuned to what happens within, while extroverts focus externally on the world around them.[3] Both types naturally want to spend more time in the "real world" but disagree on which that is—the external world of experience or the inner world of thought.

Researchers generally agree that introverts and extroverts are born, not made. While one's tendency may shift over time (people tend to become more introverted as they get older),[4] they don't *choose* to be one type or the other. Studies estimate that one-third to one-half of us fall on the introverted end of the spectrum.[5] Men are ever so slightly more likely to be introverted than women.[6]

As far as personality distinctions go, introversion versus extroversion is an important one. Scientist J. D. Higley calls introversion and extroversion (or, as he phrases it, "inhibition and boldness") "the north and south of temperament."[7] These traits affect the very core of who we are.

Understanding the Differences

While we all need to spend time introverting and extraverting (yes, these are appropriate verbs), our innate preference is reflected in our brain chemistries. If you're an introvert and you've ever had a baffling conversation with your extroverted roommate and thought, *My brain just doesn't work like that*, you're absolutely right. Your brain doesn't work like that.

Introverts and extroverts are literally wired differently. Scientists have discovered measurable physiological differences between the two groups that affect everything from how quickly they think on their feet to how their bodies react to caffeine.[8]

Extroverts think faster than introverts, processing information in less time. Extroverts can pull this off because information travels a shorter pathway through their brains. The pathway is shorter because that information bypasses parts of the brain that introverts rely on more heavily. A shorter pathway equals faster processing time, and this faster processing time accounts for many of the observable differences between the two types. The nervous systems of extroverts and introverts also function differently from each other. Introverts prefer the sympathetic side of the nervous system, the side responsible for the "rest and digest" mode. Extroverts more frequently use the parasympathetic side of the nervous system, the side responsible for the "fight-or-flight" response. Unsurprisingly, this results in different behaviors.

Introverts and extroverts are quite different when it comes to risk-taking. Extroverts are more responsive to dopamine than introverts, which means they're more likely to take big risks and enjoy doing it. They crave stimulation, whether that comes in the form of lights and sound or social interaction. But introverts, quite literally, prefer the quiet. They tend to have a more developed prefrontal cortex, the area of the brain responsible for abstract thought and decision-making.

Morning rituals for introverts versus extroverts can look very different too. We're talking about coffee, of course. The caffeine in a cup of joe is a boon to extroverts and often a burden to their quieter counterparts. Research shows that caffeine boosts extroverts' performance but hinders introverts' productivity. Introverts simply don't need the additional stimulation caffeine delivers.[9]

Extroverts and introverts are truly different on a physiological level, and those differences play out in real life. Introverts, with their preference for the inner world, need regular periods of quiet alone time to feel like their best selves (ideally) or a functional human being (realistically). For many introverts, that means a solitary walk, a long run, or some time with a good book. They need regular retreats into their own inner worlds to stay healthy, happy, and sane.

Extroverts are the opposite: they adore stimulation. Without it, they feel just as drained and exhausted as an introvert who is forced to talk all day long. These are the people who organize raucous Saturday paintball games or margarita night for twenty. Extroverts build lots of social interaction into the rhythm of their lives, often without even thinking about it. Instead of quiet, they need energetic conversation. Instead of enjoying a solitary walk, they need to take a break in a crowded park. When they're feeling tired, they need to phone a friend.

The introversion/extroversion divide affects everything from a person's risk tolerance to their patience level to their conflict management style to whether they'd talk about their recent bikini wax in mixed company. Your dad who researches every Honda for sale in five states before making his purchase? Probably an introvert. Your friend who loves roller coasters? Probably an extrovert. Your sister who spends ten minutes in the cereal aisle debating which box to buy? Probably an introvert. Your spouse who can't stand to spend the weekend at home, relaxing—the one who wants to go *do* things? Probably an extrovert. Your child who takes *forever* to figure out what to say next, who has a crazy-long mental runway? Introvert.

While these differences may make it sound as though identifying your type would be easy, that's not always the case.

What Makes Things Difficult

When confronted with descriptions of an introvert and an extrovert, many people find it easy to type themselves because they instinctively recognize which world is their real world: either the introvert's inner world of ideas or the extrovert's external world of action. They know if they prefer to turn inward or turn outward, if they prefer the quiet or the stimulating. Others, though, aren't so sure about their type. They see characteristics of both in themselves, which makes it difficult to pick just one.

Relax—there's no such thing as a pure introvert or a pure extrovert. Jung himself said no one person is all one type or the other: "Such a man would be in a lunatic asylum."[10]

We all spend time introverting and extraverting; it's part of being human. We spend time with our thoughts, in our own heads, and we spend time focusing on the external world around us. We don't have to plan for this or think about it much; it happens automatically. In this sense, we are all ambiverts. But, according to Jung,[11] we are all *primarily* oriented one way or the other. We can't be both. We are fundamentally either focused outward or focused inward.

If you see both introvert and extrovert characteristics in yourself, how do you figure out which you are? It's not always easy, because appearances can be deceiving. Let's explore what you need to pay attention to in order to figure out your type.

Undercover Extroverts, and Introverts in Disguise

Extroverts don't spend all their time extraverting, and introverts don't always look like introverts. Here's a case in point. A friend of mine spends many Friday nights out clubbing with her musician husband, dressed in tight pants and five-inch heels, rocking out to bands amid large, noisy crowds. To an outsider, that's a decidedly extroverted pursuit. If she was trying to type herself, she could point to those Friday nights and say, "I couldn't be an introvert—no way!"

But my friend calls those evenings out her "hobby," not her "lifestyle." She hits the noisy clubs because it's important to someone she loves, and she's learned to embrace the fun of it a couple nights a month. What you *don't* see is my friend playing the homebody the rest of the weekend, reading books, making soup, and watching movies—embracing her more preferred brand of quiet. After spending a Friday night out in the external world with its people, lights, and sounds, she's more than ready to retreat to her own "real world" of her thoughts.

I relate to this, as I can pass for an outgoing extrovert at the right kind of gathering. I'm often among the last to leave a party because once I get there I have such a good time; I truly love interesting conversation with interesting people. However, as much as I enjoy those kinds of events, I find them enormously draining. At the end of the night, I'm aching to return to my real world, my inner world of thought. I jokingly say I need two cups of tea and a hundred pages of a good novel to recover from a boisterous night out, but I'm really not kidding. After a night on the town, I need to recharge my battery—by myself.

However, my extroverted friend—the one who will close down the party with me—will go home and tell her husband all about her night out to prolong the evening, feeling high on life. If you had observed us at the party, you would have thought our temperaments appeared quite similar. But my extroverted friend doesn't leave drained. She leaves energized from the rush of spending all night in *her* real world—the external world of people and conversation.

Or picture this: my extroverted author friend is currently racing to meet a deadline for her next novel. She usually prefers a packed social calendar but is in full-on monk mode, spending eleven hours a day locked in her office, just herself and her computer and her dog (but she kicks even him out if he starts distracting her). If you saw her at work, you would think there's no way she could be an extrovert, but you would be wrong. She's an extrovert spending an unusual amount of time introverting because her work demands it, and she's decided it's worth it. (Although, in her own words, "When it's over, I'm going to party like it's 1999—for a month.")

Appearances can be deceiving, but your mental state, feelings, and sometimes even physical reactions will key you in to which is *your* real world, the external world "out there" or the internal world of your thoughts.

Putting This Information to Work in Your Own Life

We all have a preferred ratio of introverting to extraverting. The question to ask yourself is, Which do I do more of: introverting or extraverting? If you can answer that question, *that's terrific*. If you can't, take an assessment.[12] Talk to a few friends about how they see you. And spend some time observing yourself and thinking through your behavior.

When you're determining your type, it's crucial to pay attention to how certain activities affect you, both *in* the moment and *after* the moment. The right questions to ask yourself include, How do I feel while I'm introverting and extraverting? Afterward, do I feel exhausted or energized?

Stacking the Deck in Your Favor

Once you understand yourself, you can stop fighting your natural tendencies and plan for them instead.

I'm a sociable introvert. I enjoy coffee dates and Christmas parties and weddings and neighborhood picnics. I love noisy family dinners and hosting playdates and chatting with other parents on the baseball sidelines. I get a little restless when I don't get regular doses of social interaction. But when I get out of balance—when I spend too much time extraverting, according to my personal definition of "too much"—*I am useless*. When I ignore the warning signs and keep extraverting until I enter the Overtalked Introvert Danger Zone, I get totally overwhelmed and borderline rude and can barely string sentences together. I wish I were exaggerating.

This happened to me recently, and the memory is still fresh and painful. Not long ago, I spent a holiday weekend away from my family, holed up with a few fellow writers who were all facing imminent deadlines and needed focused time away to work.

I spent many hours that weekend by myself, just me and my work. But I also spent many enjoyable hours talking. Talking *a lot*. Many, many hours of talking. I was dangerously close to the Overtalked Introvert Danger Zone.

After four days away, spent talking and writing and talking some more, I was counting on the solo three-hour drive home to restore my equilibrium, because my family had dinner plans that night, plans I was really looking forward to. I wasn't sure if it was wise to try to cram anything else into our holiday weekend, but I really wanted it to work. So, propelled by magical thinking, my husband and I scheduled a barbecue with good friends I was desperate to see.

I was so happy to be there, and it was so good to see everyone, but my brain refused to cooperate. If it had had the energy left to put together a coherent sentence, it would have said, "I refuse to cooperate until you take me home and let me read my hundred pages in peace." I was drained. I was exhausted. And as much as I wanted to be there, I would have done everyone a favor if I'd just stayed home. Nobody likes to feel like they're getting the leftovers, but that's all I had to offer—and it was obvious.

Realizations that arise from these out-of-the-ordinary experiences change the way I approach my everyday life. I don't live in an introverted paradise. I have a large family, and my house can get kind of rowdy. I've had to learn to carve out times of peace and quiet, to help my kids learn to (at least try) not talk to me when I'm reading, and to avoid talking on the phone when my mental and emotional batteries are in need of recharging. I've embraced the power of the long run and the short walk. I've become a big believer in a well-timed video for the kids so I can grab some downtime for myself. And I keep a close eye on the calendar to make sure my balance is right between introverting and extraverting, between noisy and quiet, between seeing friends and seeing nobody but myself.

Note that I keep saying *my* balance. We're all different in this regard, and it's up to you to figure out what *your* balance looks like.

Once you understand what you need, whether you're an extrovert or an introvert, you can structure your days around what you need to thrive—or, at the very least, survive. Because, let's be honest, some days that's the best we can hope for.

Developing an Arsenal of Coping Strategies

Sometimes the balance of introverting and extraverting doesn't fall exactly the way we want it to. Of course, we know it's not always possible to get exactly what we need, exactly when we need it. A drained introvert can't always escape to a quiet place for a little while. A drained extrovert won't always have a friend (or stranger!) handy for the needed interaction of a lively chat. But that doesn't mean all is lost.

When the world around you—whether on a macro level or in your small business or family—has norms that aren't friendly to your type or you are in a situation that's poorly situated to your temperament, it can be easy to go with the flow and deny yourself the things you need. Especially if you don't even realize you need them. But if you can identify what you need and tweak the situation accordingly, maybe you can save yourself some pain and suffering.

My friend Ashley is an extrovert who homeschools her three children. She's surrounded by people all day, which might at first blush sound like extrovert heaven. But after years of doing this, she realized that while she was talking all the time, she was starving for adult conversation. At first she felt helpless. Without quitting homeschooling, how much control did she really have over the situation? But over time, she started making little changes to better meet her needs as an extrovert.

For example, she joins a friend a few mornings a week to walk and talk. She sets a reminder to phone a friend every day after lunch to get her conversation fix. She deliberately goes to the grocery store during busy hours so she'll bump into more people. (If you're an introvert, you're probably dying just reading that.) She keeps a steady schedule of coffee dates and girls' nights out. These aren't huge changes, but they have made a big difference in how Ashley feels about her life right now.

Another friend of mine is a talented seamstress. Kim owns a business, and due to the nature of her work, she spends large chunks of time alone designing products, making marketing plans, and fulfilling orders. This would be heaven—for an introvert. As an extrovert, Kim loves her work but craves human interaction, the bustle of activity, and seeing friends on a regular basis. Interestingly, Kim didn't really struggle with meeting her extrovert needs until her family moved to my town. Here, they bought a house on a quiet cul-de-sac in the suburbs. Before the move, they lived on Main Street (really) in Small Town, USA. Kim's sewing room faced a bustling street, and whenever she needed a people fix, all she had to do was wander outside.

Kim has learned over the years how to feed her extroverted nature while sticking with the work she loves. This means taking an exercise break with a buddy (we often catch up on each others' news while logging a few miles) or working in a coffee shop so she's at least *around* people for a while. It's not the ideal situation for an extrovert. Sometimes Kim fantasizes about getting a "real job" again—the kind with an office and coworkers and a watercooler to gather around to talk about last night's episode of whatever—but the perks of being her own boss are pretty great. So as long as she consciously meets her people quota every week, she finds it a workable compromise.

Tending to your nature will look different in different seasons and situations in your life, but the underlying principles remain the same. What is draining you? (Perhaps you're exhausted because you've been with people all day.) What can you do to boost your odds of recharging on a regular basis? (Maybe you could drive home from work in total silence or put in a DVD for the kids and then go into your room and close the door.) Sometimes coming up with a workable solution is a real brain bender. But more often, it's easy to take steps in the right direction—once you figure out what the right direction is.

Places Have Personalities Too

It's not just people who can be introverted or extroverted. I first encountered the idea that places can have their own personalities in Adam McHugh's book *Introverts in the Church*,[13] and, whoa, was it eye-opening. Adam explains that some places and organizations—such as the American evangelical churches that he focuses on in his book—slant toward extroversion. Generally speaking, evangelical churches in America have more extroverted qualities than introverted ones. This extroverted personality puts extroverts at ease but can make introverts feel a little overwhelmed—or worse, as though they don't belong at all.

For years, my family attended a large nondenominational church with a decidedly extroverted feel. When we entered the sanctuary a few minutes before the Sunday morning service began, the place would be humming with conversation like a crowded cocktail party. Near the beginning of each service, we were instructed to greet all the people sitting around us by shaking hands and saying good morning. (A number of introverted friends have confessed to being chronically, strategically late to escape this expectation.) Congregants would routinely take the stage to share deeply personal stories in front of thousands of strangers. Members were encouraged to invite their neighbors into their homes for meals and Bible study. These things were much easier for the extroverts than for the introverts. "Extrovert bias" is a fancy way of saying a place caters to extroverts. According to Susan Cain, this is prevalent in many Western institutions, from churches to schools to corporations.[14] I saw it in action every weekend at this large nondenominational church.

My family attended that church for many years, and understanding the personality factors at play made a big difference in my church experience while I was there. I'm introspective by nature and tend to spend a lot of time thinking (and sometimes definitely *overthinking*) through my experiences and feelings. When I feel uncomfortable in a situation, I notice and can't help but think, *What does this mean? Why am I feeling this way?* I can't tell you just how awful it is to get that uncomfortable feeling *in church*. I'm shuddering just thinking about it.

Understanding personality a little better took a lot of the pressure off those uncomfortable moments. Why did I always feel a little ill walking into a Sunday school class? It wasn't a message from above; I felt ill because it was like being late to a party in full swing. (I learned to arrive a little earlier, before the class got crowded and loud.) Why did some of the testimonies make me queasy? Because I imagined what I would do if *I* were asked to share a deeply personal story in that setting, and introverts don't generally like to share their deeply felt emotions with strangers. Why did the meet and greet make me want to run away? The explanation was simple: I was an introvert. This straightforward reason for why I felt the way I did was such a comfort.

A few years ago, my family was on the hunt for a new church home. High on our wish list was a church near our home and, ideally, one my kids were already somewhat familiar with, so we visited churches of many different denominations. I'll never forget the Sunday I took them to an Episcopal church in our own neighborhood for the first time. We walked into the old building, and it was *quiet*. It wasn't particularly crowded. Most of the people were older than my parents; there weren't many kids in sight. The organ was playing classical music. *We just have to make it through an hour*, I thought. Over the course of that hour, we sang traditional hymns and recited traditional prayers and listened to a traditional sermon and passed the peace and participated in a rather lengthy Eucharist.

Surprise, surprise—my kids loved it. Well, at least the two introverts who were old enough to express an opinion did. "It's so peaceful," they said. "It's so beautiful inside. It's so *quiet*." It took me a little while to realize that in their minds, quiet was a good thing.

Years later, my family still happily attends an Episcopal church with an introverted personality. We didn't choose it for that reason alone. Many factors go into choosing a church (or a school or a job). But we paid close attention to the personalities of the churches we visited and asked ourselves, How do we see personality at play here? What would it mean for us to be a part of this place?

When You're Feeling out of Your Comfort Zone

Some places have an extroverted flavor, and some have an introverted one. Yet I'm constantly surprised to see biases pop up in places I would have expected to be pretty neutral.

My oldest son is an ardent baseball fan and holds his own on the field. His coach last season awarded player positions based on how much "enthusiasm" his players showed. "Who wants to play shortstop? Jump up and down and make some noise!" he would yell. But my son is extremely introverted, and he preferred to show his enthusiasm through his work ethic, his conscientiousness, and the extra drills he completed on his own time. He didn't scream and shout or jump up and down, so he didn't get picked. He wasn't playing as much as he should have based on his ability.

My husband and I realized what was going on, and we were able to talk about it with our son throughout the course of the season. We discussed what extroverts bring to the table, such as the ability to make their presence felt, as that coach knew well. As a group, extroverts are outspoken and outgoing. They think well on their feet and can handle—and even thrive on—social pressure. We wouldn't want to live in a world without extroverts! Introverts bring many important qualities to the table too. However, those qualities are more easily overlooked or underappreciated in an extroverted culture.

As a parent, the thought of my kid being passed over because of his personality guts me, which was great motivation to open an ongoing conversation with him about what it means to advocate for yourself, whether you're thirteen or thirty-seven. When is it worth speaking up, even if it feels uncomfortable? (Perhaps if the position of shortstop is on the line.) How can you make your performance stand out, even if you dread the spotlight? (Maybe by saying, "Hey, coach, I've been practicing hard. I hope you notice today.")

We couldn't change the coach's bias (well, not without getting banned from the bleachers with the other parents who get too rowdy on the sidelines), but we could at least understand what was happening, explain it to our son, and help him adjust his behavior accordingly. It's not a perfect solution, but it's a move in the right direction.

Extrovert bias may be more common, but introvert bias is also a real thing. Some places definitely prefer the quieter types. I discovered a striking example of this last year when a friend surprised me with a story from her graduate school days, when she attended one of the country's premier MFA programs. I was impressed by her accomplished pedigree and told her so. She's a great writer, but she doesn't write the kind of fiction that literature professors usually fawn over (at least not in class).

She confessed that I wasn't wrong; she had definitely been a fish out of water back in grad school. She showed up at her very serious school and immediately set to doing what she does best—plan a good cocktail party. Her fellow students thought they'd spend their weekend nights reading—or, at the very most, discussing—novels, but she was determined to lure them to her apartment for drinks and food and chitchat.

When I imagine my friend at grad school, I picture her as Elle Woods, as played by Reese Witherspoon in the movie *Legally Blonde*, heading off to Harvard Law School with her fashion merchandising degree in hand. Elle Woods is five-foot-one, blonde, and, well, *fictional*, and my friend is five-foot-ten, brunette, and has an actual birth certificate, but they both had that outsider thing going on in their chosen educational institutions. Plus, they both rose to the top *and* had a great time at school.

The literati didn't take my friend seriously at first; she was too bubbly to be talented, or something like that. She was greeted with pretty much the same reception that Elle got at Harvard ("What are *you* doing *here*?"), but in the end, she found a way to meet her extroverted needs in an introverted place—*and* land a publisher.

Tending to Your Relationships

Because we live in a world with many other people—people we work with, live with, and care about—we need to be not only smart about meeting our own needs but also gracious about *their* needs. It's important to know our own personality types and what we need because of them, but we also have to learn to be flexible. Remember, the people we love and live with have needs too.

Take the holiday season, for example. I love getting together with my extended family, especially during this time of year. My husband and I take our four kids to my parents' house, his parents' house, and, if we're lucky, my grandmother's house as well. I wouldn't miss any of these visits for the world.

However, as an introvert, the successive days of big family gatherings take their toll on me. As much as I love seeing everyone, the cumulative effect of these get-togethers is exhausting. If I'm not smart about managing my energy during this time of year, I'm not able to enjoy my visits with family. (Good books, hot tea, and Netflix can go a long way toward getting an introvert through the holiday season in one piece. I don't think it's a coincidence that the big holiday shows often release on Thanksgiving and Christmas—the networks know we need a break from all that togetherness!)

Sometimes our wishes directly oppose those of our loved ones. One Friday night not too long ago, my husband returned home from a work trip to Seattle. He's an introvert, like me, and he'd spent four straight days in meetings and at work dinners. When his flight landed, he wanted to drive straight home and spend the evening eating pizza and hanging out with his family in his pajamas. However, while he was out and about in Seattle, I'd been feeling cooped up at home. A good friend was hosting a family cookout the night he got home, and I was ready to go out!

In a situation like that, not everyone gets their first choice. Someone has to give. Our personalities don't provide the answer to these decisions, but they can serve as useful guides. Personality is just one of many factors to consider, but it's an important one.

Years ago, I probably would have just accepted his answer (in typical Enneagram type Nine style, which we'll talk about in chapter 9), but I've learned enough about my personality to at least sometimes understand the reasons why I want to do certain things. I didn't give up. Will and I talked it through and found out he had a *slight* preference for staying in. However, I felt strongly about going out. So we went. (Just last week I wanted to go someplace and he didn't—notice a pattern here?—but that time he *really* wanted to stay home, and I didn't feel nearly as strongly about it, so we skipped the thing.)

We are all different, even different in our expressions of introversion or extroversion. By understanding ourselves and how we might be different from others, we can better appreciate other people and the way they are wired. And with practice and experience, through trial and error, we'll get better at making the right decisions for ourselves, as well as for the people around us.

A Different Kind of Normal

Now that I understand more about introversion and extroversion, I understand why my mom gets a big kick out of drawing connections between people. It's her nature. She loves constant human interaction and bringing people together to *talk, talk, talk* in order to facilitate more of it. She'll want to tell me that my new neighbor was married in 1989 to her old sorority sister's cousin's dentist's dog walker or introduce me to her third-grade teacher's daughter when we bump into them at the mall. I really don't care, but I listen. Because while I may not care about her old sorority sister's cousin's dentist's dog walker, I care about my mom. And these are the things that matter to *her*.

Understanding our personalities doesn't eliminate the tension that results when people with different needs, motivations, and preferences come together or, especially, live together. But understanding things beneath the surface—*why* people act the way they act and prefer the things they prefer—helps us at least make sense of what's going on. These people are not out to get us or trying to ruffle our feathers; they're just different—a different kind of normal.

3

Too Hot To Handle

highly sensitive people

It was Thursday, and I was screaming.

Again.

I don't exactly have a fiery personality. When I tell my friends—even my close friends, the ones who hear about my embarrassing moments and flat-on-my-face failures—stories about losing my cool with my kids, they say they can't imagine me ever getting angry. Apparently, the vibe I project is *mellow*. But had these friends been at my house on a Thursday morning circa 2007, they wouldn't have doubted my inner dragon.

Back then I was a stay-at-home mom to three kids. At least I was on Thursdays. I worked part-time three days a week and had outside obligations on "other days." But on Thursdays, the kids and I had nowhere to be and nothing to do at any certain time.

I'm kind of a homebody. I *love* spending time at home. I assumed "nowhere to be" and "nothing to do" were good things. Yet Thursdays and I never got along.

On Thursday mornings, when it was just the kids and me at home, I would brew an extra cup of coffee (nowhere to be!) and dress comfy (nothing to do!). And then—since I was home, for once—I'd take a good hard look at my house to see what needed cleaning and tidying. And once I saw it, I had to *do* something about it.

My house wasn't typically a total disaster, but with three kids in a smallish space, a good bit of stuff was often lying about. I would start by cleaning the surfaces; that was fine. As I would sweep the papers and crayons and small toys—*so many small toys*—out from under the sofa, I could feel the tension start to rise. When I would progress into the bedroom my two young daughters shared and see, with my Thursday morning let's-get-this-mess-under-control-right-now eyes, the tiny scraps of paper and shreds of fabric and hair ties and beads on every ever-loving surface, I would get twitchy. Then I would ask the kids for help and they all would start telling me, at the same time, why it wasn't their fault there were no clear surfaces in the house. Meanwhile, the dog, excited by the ruckus, would inevitably start barking, escalating the family chaos.

That's the point at which my usually mild-mannered self would become completely overwhelmed by the situation at hand and lose it. (This is the part with the screaming. It was ugly. I'll spare you the details.)

At the time, I had no idea what was going on. Eventually, I realized that something about Thursdays put me over the edge. I thought it might be that I wasn't cut out to be a stay-at-home mom, not even one day a week. (Nope.) I hypothesized that I lost my temper because I hated cleaning that much. (Not that, either.) It wasn't either of these things. I finally, *finally* realized the "problem" wasn't a problem at all. Instead, the cause was my highly tuned nervous system. It was completely overwhelmed by the clutter and noise of Thursdays—but I could actually do something to make the day more manageable, if I chose to do so.

If you're reading this, the odds are about one in five that you are a highly sensitive person (HSP)—that is, you have a highly sensitive nervous system. High sensitivity is a hardwired physiological trait that affects 15–20 percent of the population, across species, not just in humans.[1] These people aren't touchy or overly emotional; high sensitivity describes people whose nervous systems are more receptive to stimuli than those of the general population. This means they are more attuned to subtleties in their surroundings and are more easily overwhelmed by highly stimulating environments. Their internal "radar" for detecting external stimuli is quite good, but it takes energy to keep that radar operational, which can be exhausting.

What You Need to Know about Highly Sensitive People

You know from experience or from reading this book that human interaction drains introverts. In a similar way, sensory input— sights, smells, sounds, emotional stimulation—drains highly sensitive people. Though this trait is often mistaken as a subset of introversion, it's not. People of all personality types can be sensitive, whether introverts or extroverts. Although introverts are more likely to be highly sensitive, a full 30 percent of highly sensitive people are extroverts.[2]

I'm an HSP to the core. I avoid violent imagery (I abandoned reading Elaine Aron's *The Highly Sensitive Person* on my first try because—in typical HSP fashion—I couldn't handle the frequent references to sexual abuse). I'm very empathetic, and I feel as though my head will explode when two people try to talk to me at the same time. I have difficulty making dinner while the counter is cluttered with the morning's dishes. I lose my mind when someone is singing while the radio is playing a different song. Watching the news makes me want to assume the fetal position and never get up.

I'm raising kids who are highly sensitive as well. Highly sensitive children (HSCs) are more prone to be bothered by scratchy clothes and itchy socks, unfamiliar tastes and loud noises, daily transitions and changes in routine. The younger an HSC is, the less they'll be able to articulate what exactly is going on. Instead, their baffled parent, friend, or caregiver will be left wondering what is different about them, why they cry all the time, why they can't just chill out.

What Sets HSPs Apart

If you're highly sensitive, you'll probably recognize yourself in the description of an HSP immediately. HSPs—who have a strong tendency for self-reflection—easily resonate with their own description. From childhood, they may have startled easily, struggled with big changes of any sort, hated noisy places, been exceptionally picky about the texture of their food, cried when bothered by the seams in their socks or the tags in their T-shirts, and seemed strongly attuned to the feelings of others. As adults, they are strikingly intuitive, inclined toward perfectionism, sensitive to pain, and apt to notice subtleties in their environments. High sensitivity manifests in a wide variety of ways. While all of the above traits are telltale signs of high sensitivity, not all HSPs react to the same stimuli.

What sets HSPs apart? For one, the brains of HSPs process information, such as that brought in through the five senses, more thoroughly than nonsensitive types. They also process experiences more deeply than those who lack the trait. They dwell on things more and longer than the rest of the population. They catch subtle cues that others miss. Their emotional reaction is stronger—to the positive *and* negative.

But it's not just the brains of HSPs that are different. Their whole bodies seem uniquely designed to detect more information. Their reflexes are faster; they're more sensitive to pain, medicines, and stimulants; they have more allergies than non-sensitive types and more active immune systems. Compared to nonsensitives, their reactive systems seem turbocharged.

I love the way Elaine Aron describes highly sensitive people in her book *The Highly Sensitive Child*, drawing on a childhood visit to an orange-packing plant. She writes, "I liked the ingenious invention that moved the oranges down a shaking conveyor belt until they fell into one of three sized slots—small, medium, or large. I now use that experience as a way to describe the brains of HSCs. Instead of having three slots for processing what comes down the conveyor belt to them, they have fifteen slots, for making very fine distinctions. And all goes well until too many oranges come down the belt at once. Then you have a huge jam up."[3]

Those "jam ups" happen when an HSP becomes overstimulated. For highly sensitive people, the world often feels as though it's just too much. Too overwhelming. They're never just a little hungry or a little tired. They feel things strongly. Everything is a big deal. And though all of us can be overstimulated at one time or another, HSPs are especially prone to it. When HSPs get overwhelmed, their overworked nervous systems shut down because they can't take the strain any longer.

Common Triggers for Highly Sensitive People

While different sorts of HSPs have various sensitivities, there are certain common themes.

1. *Noise.* An early clue that our child was an HSC was his reaction to his first fireworks show around age two. All the other children around us were mesmerized by the colorful display. Our kid burst into tears at the first boom.

   HSPs frequently dislike loud noises and nonstop noise of any sort. This could mean rock concerts, the buzz of a cocktail party, or coffee hour at church. Similarly, talking for a long period of time can be exceptionally draining.

2. *Clutter.* Messy spaces are draining for many HSPs because there's too much visual input. Although I would never describe myself as a neatnik, I've noticed that keeping my house tidy (or tidy enough) keeps my metaphorical fuel tank full. If you're an HSP, clear kitchen counters do a lot for inner calm.

3. *Texture.* In addition to sounds, textures can also feel invasive and irritating. This is often a parent's first clue that their child is highly sensitive. The child may express discomfort with clothing tags, seams in socks, or, in my own child's case, the unpleasant stiffness of silk-screened T-shirts. Often, HSCs' actual physical bodies are sensitive.

4. *People.* People are interesting, varied, and stimulating, which means they can certainly be overwhelming.

5. *Consecutive errands/meetings/appointments.* Nonstop go, go, go wears out HSPs because of the constant (and varied) input without any time in between to recover.

6. *Big feelings.* HSPs process information more deeply, including emotional information. For example, listening to a girlfriend share her troubles can make nonsensitive friends feel just fine but can be completely overwhelming for HSPs. And HSPs can feel overwhelmed by their own emotions. Sorrow, joy, fatigue, anxiety—there's no such thing as a little bit sad or a little bit happy or a little bit tired. HSPs don't feel things halfway.

7. *Information overload.* Taking in lots of information in a short time period makes HSPs feel overwhelmed.

8. *Media.* In addition to the information overload aspect, media can also trigger big feelings, and the combination is brutal. HSPs are especially vulnerable to crumpling when faced with nonstop coverage of a devastating event. Many HSPs choose to abstain from news sites (and stay off social media in the wake of big events). They don't do it because they're cold and callous; they do it because they can't bear the pain of the whole world.

9. *Decisions.* Decisions are a major source of energy drain for HSPs (and many introverts). Everyone experiences decision fatigue to some degree. But for HSPs, who are better able to perceive the nuances and subtle implications of every possible way forward, decision fatigue kicks in sooner and lasts longer.

It's not possible to skirt every trigger, but being cognizant of their triggers helps HSPs not be surprised by them and allows sensitive types to avoid or moderate such triggers when possible. But it's not until HSPs understand what high sensitivity means—and how it affects them and those around them—that they can begin to actually do something about it.

Putting This Information to Work in Your Own Life

Once you understand high sensitivity, you can recognize almost instantly if you—or someone you love, live with, or work with—is an HSP. If you're not sure, take one of Elaine Aron's wonderful free assessments.[4] Armed with a little knowledge, you can be more prepared to deal with your highly sensitive responses to the world.

Even if you are an HSP and don't feel as though you need to take drastic action, the diagnosis is its own sort of cure. Simple understanding brings instant relief. You understand that you're not alone, and you're not crazy. And in addition to bringing relief, knowing you are an HSP can bring a new appreciation for not only the hardships of bearing the trait but also the benefits.

Now, let's take a look at how to move forward.

What You Can and Can't Change about High Sensitivity

A common thread throughout this book is to identify what you can and cannot change about yourself so you can make smart decisions moving forward.

The first thing you need to know about highly sensitive people is that their nervous systems are what they are. People can grow and develop in countless ways, but there is no volume knob they can access to turn down their nervous systems' naturally elevated response to stimuli. This trait is hardwired.

This means that they're probably going to cry more than nonsensitive types, no matter what. They're going to be more sensitive to criticism than you might see as "reasonable." They're going to be reluctant to see that new slasher movie or hit up all the roller coasters at the local amusement park. They don't want to eat at that new popular but noisy restaurant in town. Many corporate team-building activities will feel like "too much" for them. They can't change these things about themselves.

It's not possible for HSPs to avoid every trigger or always get what they need (if only!). But that doesn't mean—I'm speaking as an HSP here—we have no control over the things that drive us bonkers.

Let me offer a personal example. I've long known that when all four of my kids are talking to me at the same time, it burns my fuel at about eighty times the usual rate. All those voices and ideas are way too much input for my HSP brain to sort. (Remember those oranges?) Kids make noise; I have four of them. I can't change that (nor would I want to—*most days*). But I can change how I understand and respond to that situation. The problem isn't my kids; it's the noise and the way it's coming at me fast and furious. I've found everyone is happier when I ask (tell, demand, require) my kids to speak to me one at a time before I reach "situation critical level," instead of flipping my lid and screaming at them to "just stop talking already because I'm losing my ever-loving mind!" Not that I've ever done that. *Ahem.*

I can't change my nature, but that doesn't mean I can't change the situation.

Giving HSPs What They Need

The bad news for HSPs is that they have many things draining their fuel tanks. The good news is that they can control some, maybe even many, of those factors.

I've lost count of how many emails I've gotten from people saying something like "I thought I wasn't cut out for family life, but it turns out I'm just an HSP. What a relief!" Time after time, these people have told me they were afraid that something was wrong with them because no one else seemed to react to everyday life events the way they did (that is, *strongly*). Once they understood high sensitivity and recognized it in themselves, they no longer felt as though they were a freak or all alone or damaged. Knowing they were dealing with something both specific and manageable—not to mention, not in their heads—gave them a new sense of hope. They were able to develop an action plan to make sure they got what they needed moving forward.

And what do HSPs need?

More than anything, HSPs need white space, both literal and metaphorical. In a sea of input, HSPs need some rest from the tidal wave of sensory input. This is so their brains can sort through the backload of oranges to clear those inevitable jam ups.

Many HSPs intuitively know what they need, but for others, it's helpful to see a punch list of the qualities they would do well to seek out in their day-to-day life. The following are high-priority items for HSPs.

1. *Quiet.* Noise is a big deal for HSPs. In fact, noise is so problematic that Elaine Aron calls it "the bane of the HSP's existence."[5] HSPs are more sensitive to noises of all sorts than the nonsensitive majority, and they have an extremely difficult time filtering it out to focus on other things.

   Whether they are working in a busy office or staying home with ten kids, HSPs need some noise-free zones in their day. (If you're in a position where that's not possible right now, I'm sorry. I've been there. It will get better, but until then, give yourself some grace because you're in a trying situation.) Many HSPs in this situation have found that automating some systems so they can talk less and have a little more quiet is very valuable. (Two mundane examples: if Tuesday is always taco night, there's no need to decide or debate what's for dinner. If approved snacks for kids are always in the fridge's snack drawer or on a certain pantry shelf, a ten-minute conversation about what's approved for snack is unnecessary.)

While it may be tempting to listen to podcasts, audiobooks, or music when you're alone on a walk, in the car, or doing the dishes, the HSP brain needs time to rest, reflect, and recharge.

2. *Peaceful, clutter-free environments*. Not always, obviously. But when HSPs need to recharge, environment matters.

3. *Privacy*. If you're not highly sensitive, you may think it's quite nice to sit at the kitchen counter and quietly do your work side by side with your HSP spouse or friend or roommate. But you, as a human being, could be putting their nervous system on alert just by virtue of your presence. You may not notice the quiet clatter of your keyboard, but they do. You may not realize you're sighing or laughing, but they do. When HSPs need to focus, they often prefer to work (or read or walk or think) alone.

4. *Downtime*. More than most, HSPs need to be deliberate about resting and recharging at regular intervals. When you need to recharge, make sure you do something that actually fills your tank. For example, HSPs may love catching up

with a friend on the phone, but it's quite possible this will drain them instead of filling them up. Instead of listening to a podcast, HSPs may be better off spending twenty minutes with a good book and a cup of coffee. For you, that may mean going for a run or a walk through the woods or knitting or taking apart a radio.

5. *Minimal information intake.* HSPs may need to limit the amount of information they take in at certain times. They also need to be especially careful about not making their tech tools—especially their smartphones—instruments of their own destruction. Our era, as in all eras, has its share of tragedy. But in stark contrast to other eras, our hyper-connectivity means detaching ourselves from the swirl of twenty-four-hour news coverage on the latest crisis can be difficult. HSPs are more likely to be exhausted because of the sheer amount of information coming in from all directions. As a general rule, I don't check email, Twitter, or Facebook when I'm supposed to be taking a "break." The last thing my brain needs is additional stimulation via email or social media.

6. *Routine.* Embracing routine is helpful for many HSPs. Smooth routines make for fewer decisions, which is good because decisions tax HSPs' mental energy more than that of non-HSPs. We're all vulnerable to decision fatigue, but HSPs are even more so. Consistent routines offer the bonus of less talking. This is a bonus because talking zaps their energy.

7. *Boundaries.* Good boundaries are crucial for the care and keeping of intuitive types. The same inner radar that lets them "know" things about people and places can also

work against them, causing them to adeptly take in negative energy. This can be so draining that Aron advises HSPs to make setting good boundaries an explicit goal.

Particular Concerns about Parenting a Highly Sensitive Child

It may take a while for parents to realize that some typical activities most kids consider fun are torture for highly sensitive children. My HSC hated the echo-y indoor play places at fast-food restaurants and the animated movies from Pixar and Disney every other kid seemed to love. To my dismay, one of the places my young HSC hated most passionately was children's church. When he was young, the large evangelical church we attended had an equally large children's program. The children's room was packed with throngs of people, exciting games, blaring music, and flashing lights. My friends' nonsensitive children loved it.

But this environment that nonsensitive children experienced as fun was literally painful to the sensitive child. For every nine kids having a blast, one was huddled in the corner with his hands over his ears. The place was overwhelming. The people, the lights, and the noise combined for a nonstop assault on their senses.

If you are the parent of an HSC, be aware that your child's specific needs must be managed just as any other highly sensitive person's needs would be, but the fact that it's *your* child brings an extra sense of responsibility.

If you suspect your child is highly sensitive, an official assessment (such as Elaine Aron's good and free one, which I mentioned earlier) will help you identify your child's specific triggers. In most cases, that knowledge combined with a hefty dose of common sense and ingenuity will help you and your child tremendously. Professional attention is not usually required, although it never hurts to ask your pediatrician if you're concerned. High sensitivity is a natural and normal trait.

You can be a great parent for your HSC whether or not you're highly sensitive yourself. As we've seen at my house, each pairing has pros and cons. Because I'm highly sensitive, I understand what my HSCs are dealing with, and I intuitively know how to respond in certain situations. I have empathy up the wazoo for their struggles. My husband, Will, is not highly sensitive, and he has unique strengths when it comes to parenting our HSCs, not despite his nonsensitivity but *because* of it. (Important note: When I say "nonsensitive," I don't mean the man doesn't have feelings. I just mean he doesn't *feel* things the way the highly sensitive do.) He brings grounding and balance to our highly sensitive children. When the kids are punching my highly sensitive buttons, Will isn't fazed. And because of his nonsensitive nature, he prods our HSCs to try new things much more than I do.

All parents advocate for their children, but parents of an HSC need to learn what their individual child needs and educate the people who regularly interact with them. This is usually easier for parents who are not highly sensitive themselves. The younger the child is, the more it's appropriate to shield them from the triggers that drive them bananas, whether that means buying tag-free clothing or turning down the blaring music in their brother's room or keeping the playroom at least a *little* bit tidy or not leaving the kitchen counter continuously buried under a three-inch pile of homework and art projects, aka visual clutter. So my HSCs know what's coming next, I've asked our babysitter to let them first read to themselves the ending of a book the sitter is reading aloud, if they're asking to do so. I've asked my mom not to run four errands in a row with my kids in tow. And I've even spoken with my children's teachers about *not* making my HSC participate in activities like finger painting with condiments in class (a real example and one that gets my gag reflex going every time I think about it—talk about sensory overload!).

Parents can teach their highly sensitive children how to move in the world, equipping them to get what they need while mitigating their triggers. You and your child can learn to speak the language of high sensitivity. My HSCs, who used to feel generally flustered on a regular basis without really knowing why, have learned to specifically identify what is troubling them. They've learned to ask themselves if it might be the noise making them uncomfortable, or the bright lights, or the seams of their socks, or even playground drama at school, and to voice their concerns when appropriate.

Understanding is the greatest gift any parent can give their highly sensitive child. Don't pretend they're not different; they already know they are. To thrive, they need to acknowledge, understand, and appreciate what makes them unique—and they need you to do these things too.

The Upside of High Sensitivity

High sensitivity is a mixed bag. Sometimes HSPs feel as though they would trade places with a nonsensitive type in a heartbeat. What they wouldn't give to be able to take things in stride for once instead of always experiencing everything so strongly! But high sensitivity has its perks, and I don't think many HSPs would sacrifice them without a fight.

The bad news for HSPs is that their nervous systems are extremely sensitive. But there's good news too: their nervous systems are extremely sensitive. If you're an HSP, it may be hard to believe this is a *good* thing—at least on the days when the world is overwhelming you and you're fantasizing about moving to a cabin in the woods in Vermont by yourself—but the sensitivity that sometimes makes you want to run and hide can be a tremendous strength. Experiencing *more* does have advantages. This trait makes you a kind and caring friend, an empathetic and wise counselor, an insightful employee, and a spiritual seeker.

HSPs can be intense. They are passionate by nature, and can make others feel their passion too. They have laser-like focus and dedicate boatloads of attention to the things they care about. They're able to explore issues in depth, seeing the nuances that others miss or choose to ignore. They're extremely perceptive, picking up on all sorts of things nonsensitive types miss. They are really good at deep conversation and are eager to explore meaningful topics. And they're creative, able to turn their hyper-awareness within to generate new ideas. When we think of high sensitivity in that light, it sounds like a superpower.

As for me, I still have days when I have a hard time believing my high sensitivity is truly "normal," such as when a cheesy pop song makes me cry even though I objectively think it's stupid. Or the grating department store elevator music pushes me toward the melting point. Or my übercluttered kitchen counters threaten to overwhelm me. But learning more about my nervous system has helped me understand that although I'm outnumbered by nonsensitive types, I'm certainly not alone. And I'm just fine the way I am. Understanding myself has also helped me stop screaming on Thursday mornings—and for that, I am grateful. Wouldn't you be too?

4

Love and Other Acts of Blindness

the five love languages

For as long as I've known Will, even before we were married, his mother has sent me greeting cards for every occasion.

She loves greeting cards so much that she arranges card blitzes for her loved ones' birthdays. When her mother turned eighty, she arranged for her to receive eighty cards in the mail—from friends, yes, but also from total strangers. Her mom thought this was awesome. When a friend turned seventy, she magically received seventy cards in her mailbox, thanks to my mother-in-law, and she was delighted to get them. I didn't understand. It's just paper—and it's not as though it's paper that bears warm, personal communications. It's expensive paper, preprinted with commercial messages!

Then again, I have never been a "card person." I just don't care. Often, I'd save the cards she sent and wonder what to do with the clutter they created, or I'd toss them but feel guilty about it.

A few years back, I changed my tune. Now, I send greeting cards. (Or at least I intend to and feel like I missed an opportunity when I don't.) It wasn't my mother-in-law who changed my mind—or a friend or my husband. Gary Chapman's 1992 book *The 5 Love Languages* introduced the world to another personality framework *and* changed my mind about greeting cards.

The book and its subsequent spin-offs—love languages for men, children, teens, singles, and even members of the military— have struck a chord with readers everywhere. Chapman's books have sold ten million copies and counting. The ideas are simple and easy to grasp. They offer a framework that quickly transforms the way you see people and, subsequently—after lots of practice and intentionality—your relationships.

As we've learned in the previous chapters, various personality frameworks shed light on how people approach the world in fundamentally different ways. Each of us has a unique perspective that affects everything we do, and how we love is no exception. Like all other personality differences, innocent misunderstandings about how to express love can wreak havoc on our most important relationships. These misunderstandings put a wall between us and our loved ones, making good communication impossible.

Sometimes these misunderstandings are harmless, or even funny. When I was a teenager, my family went to Germany. Thanks to several years of high school German, my communication skills were good enough to navigate Germany's sites, restaurants, and transportation systems.

That changed the night we went out to a cozy little restaurant with a German friend in Münster. Our dinner was fantastic—

and filling—and when we were finished, our server came to our table and asked if we'd like dessert. I quickly answered—in German—that I was too full to eat anything else.

The server looked surprised; our German friend started laughing. When she caught her breath, she explained that I had just told the server I was far too pregnant to eat anything else. I was a slender, fresh-faced, fifteen-year-old girl.

My intonation was good. My words were accurate. My intentions were pure. In my head, I could see no reason why the server didn't catch my meaning. Yet I didn't say what I had meant to say—not even close, in fact.

Mine was a harmless mistake. We were talking about dessert, and a friend fluent in both languages was there to correct it. Communication breakdowns like this happen every day. However, those mistakes aren't about dessert but about our most important relationships. When it comes to love, it's crucial to understand that all of us speak languages that can feel just as different as English is from German. And when we don't even realize we're speaking different languages, we're especially vulnerable to losing the message in translation.

What You Need to Know about the Five Love Languages

Fundamentally, Chapman believes love is an action; it must be demonstrated in ways others can understand. He introduced the idea that there are five main ways people *express* love:

1. words of affirmation
2. quality time
3. giving and receiving gifts

4. acts of service

5. physical touch[1]

We all speak one of these five love languages fluently—it's our primary language. This is the language we're born with, and it's probably the language of our parents and siblings. It makes us feel loved. Most of us are fairly comfortable with a second language but less so with the remaining three.

Trouble inevitably arises when we don't realize or fail to remember that our primary language isn't the *only* language; it's one of many. And when our spouses (or children or parents or friends) speak different languages—ones we're not fluent in—we can't understand one another. Even if we're sincerely expressing love in the best way we know how, others may utterly fail to comprehend our actions. And vice versa.

This isn't anyone's fault. It's the variety of human experience that keeps things interesting. But as human beings, we all have the fundamental need to feel loved, especially by those closest to us. If we don't learn to speak a secondary language so that the ones we love can actually *feel* our love for them, then we're doomed.

Bridging the Language Barrier

Most of us can usually recognize sincere expressions of love from our loved ones. But Chapman says our emotional tanks cannot be filled unless our primary love languages are spoken.[2]

I first learned of the concept of the "emotional bank account" when Will and I were in a couples' small group at church with seven or eight other newly married couples. One night someone introduced me to a concept that has stuck with me ever since.

Imagine that we all have an internal checking account, but it's not money that's on deposit—it's love. When we receive and truly *feel* an expression of love, that's a deposit into our account. When our loved one does something (or *doesn't* do something) and it makes us feel unloved, that's a withdrawal. It became a joke in our group to verbally track deposits and withdrawals we could observe on display. When a husband would say something that was complimentary to his wife, someone would jokingly say, "Now, *there's* a deposit!" And when the opposite happened, someone would exclaim, "You'd better make sure you don't overdraw his account!"

It seemed silly. We were all young and in love, weren't we?

In fact, I remember the winter when we were regularly commenting that a certain man in our group was making lots of withdrawals from his wife's account. We always said it in jest, and it was funny and lighthearted, a sign of group camaraderie—or so we thought. I assumed that because he was outspoken about *everyone's* strengths and weaknesses—including his wife's—she accepted and maybe even liked this about him. I was stunned when, just a few months later, she told me they were getting divorced. They were the first of our friends to split up. When we met for lunch after their separation, she explained, "He said he loved me, but I never felt like he really did."

In *The 5 Love Languages*, Chapman uses a metaphor similar to the emotional bank account: the emotional love tank. He writes that we all have a vehicle that needs a certain kind of fuel. But whatever we choose to picture, whether a bank account or a vehicle, realize that being on empty is painful. Having an empty tank, or account, leaves us feeling isolated, unknown, and unappreciated. As my friend can tell you, this is devastating to any relationship.

It's essential to our emotional health that we feel adequately loved, and our emotional tanks need to be filled up for us to feel we are truly loved (even if we intellectually believe we are).

So how do we keep others' tanks full? We need to be sure we express our love *in a way our loved ones can actually receive*. This means learning to speak their primary love languages, even if they don't come naturally to us, because that is how they will best feel our love.

In any relationship—especially in marriage and family relationships—each person needs to not only know they are loved but also feel it. If we don't learn to speak a loved one's love language, then that person won't feel our love. What's worse, our failure to communicate love in a way our loved one can understand may feel so horrible that they will feel not only unloved but also as if we are deliberately *withholding* love. Not good!

Being able to speak your spouse's language ensures that both of you will continue to feel loved even when the initial high/ infatuation of falling in love fades away. (Chapman says the initial "in love" feeling lasts two years, so if you're in it for the long haul, you have to learn to speak your spouse's love language.)

On a lighter note, the love languages framework can also open your eyes to understanding more about your mate as a person: who they are, what they enjoy, what makes them "tick." And doesn't continually learning more about your spouse keep things interesting?

When learning about the five love languages, it's important to remember that love is a choice. If we don't naturally speak our loved ones' love languages, then we need to learn how to do what doesn't come naturally. And every day we need to choose to demonstrate our love to them.

The Five Love Languages Explained

To pinpoint your love language, you first need to get a feel for what each of the languages looks like. Once you do, you'll be able to spot them in action in your life and the lives of your loved ones.

Words of Affirmation

People with the primary language of words of affirmation want to hear you speak your love through compliments and appreciative words. It's not enough to show them you love them with your actions; they need to hear it spoken.

Words are incredibly important to someone with this primary love language. Imagine a realtor's focus on "location, location, location." For a person who needs words of affirmation, it's all about "words, words, words." These people love compliments, thoughtful notes, and encouraging texts. Kindness is universally important; these people crave it—and appreciate it—most of all. They need to be sincerely thanked for what they do, and they need to regularly hear the actual words *I love you*.

Quality Time

People with the primary love language of quality time best understand love in the form of undivided attention. The emphasis here is on *quality*. Not all time spent together is quality time. This doesn't typically mean a side-by-side Netflix binge. Quality time people are big on quality conversation, which involves sharing thoughts *and* feelings. They need more than to just *talk* about something; they need to talk about how you *feel* about something.

People with this primary love language often put a high value on doing quality activities together. That may be a long walk, a Saturday canoe trip, a weekend getaway, or even a basement clean-out day. Chapman calls this yearning for shared quality activities a "dialect" of quality time.

When Will and I started dating, we loved to run errands together. We still do, really, and when you find that special someone who makes the DMV tolerable, you don't let them go. Unsurprisingly, we're both big on quality time.

Giving and Receiving Gifts

People with the primary love language of receiving gifts appreciate tangible, physical symbols of love. They want something they can hold in their hands, a touchable symbol of love.

Some symbols of love are obvious—a wedding ring, an anniversary bracelet, tickets for courtside seats. But inexpensive gifts can be symbols of love—ticket stubs from your first date, a dandelion in the fist of a child, a handwritten card. The last time my husband flew to Seattle for work he brought me back a pound of coffee from my favorite Seattle coffee shop. It wasn't expensive, but it showed me he knows me, he knows what I like, and he was thinking of me even though he was three thousand miles away.

Sometimes the most important gift you can give is the gift of your physical presence, especially during a time of need. This could mean picking up a pizza on the way home or watching a show you're not particularly interested in, just because your loved one asked you to.

Acts of Service

For people with the primary love language of acts of service, talk is cheap; they want to see your love in action. They appreciate it when someone does things for them out of love. This could involve a million different acts—mowing the grass, cooking dinner, phoning the appliance repairman. It may mean a spouse takes care of the duties their partner dreads, just because they know their partner truly appreciates it.

However, this doesn't mean being a doormat or a martyr. For someone whose primary love language is acts of service, these acts must not be done out of obligation, guilt, or fear. Instead, they must be done as expressions of love to rank as deposits in their emotional bank account.

Physical Touch

Physical touch doesn't mean *only* what you think it means. (Many men make the mistake of thinking physical touch is their primary love language because of the sex thing, but Chapman makes clear that's only one aspect of it.) People with this primary love language feel connected through physical contact. Sex is one component of physical touch, obviously, but simple things like putting your hand on their arm to tell them something important, a brief hug or kiss when you say hello or goodbye, or sitting close to each other on the couch when you're watching a movie are also important to those with this primary love language.

These people often have a tactile nature and appreciate things with pleasant textures, such as cozy blankets, or tangible communication, such as handwritten notes instead of texts or emails.

Not Just for Grown-Ups

The love languages aren't just for grown-ups, either. At every age, each of us needs to know we are loved. We also need to experience that love. This is a foundational, universal human need. While the core five love languages are the same for children as for adults, the way those languages are used is different in children. (We'll talk more about this later.)

When you learn to speak your child's language, your relationship will be stronger, more relaxed, and more enjoyable.

Can Your Primary Love Language Change?

Chapman believes a person's primary love language usually stays stable over the years. But different languages can temporarily take priority in different seasons. For example, I usually cook dinner for my family and mostly enjoy doing it. But even though Will and I both are usually quality time people, while I was writing this book and my time was limited, he cooked dinner many nights, not because he particularly enjoyed the cooking but as an act of service for me.

He scheduled the appointment to repair the dishwasher and stopped at the grocery store on his way home from work. He didn't offer these acts of service because I said, "I'm too busy and don't have time," although that did happen sometimes. He knew I was swamped and asked how he could lighten my load.

While examples like these may make it appear that our love languages change over time, Chapman believes these are not permanent changes but temporary shifts due to circumstances.

Putting This Information to Work in Your Own Life

Once you understand the five love languages, you will probably recognize your primary language. But if your primary language is not immediately clear to you, ask yourself, *When I need to feel loved, what do I ask for?* Do I request a back rub, for my spouse to make dinner, for a friend to run an errand for me, or for a loved one to tell me *why* they love me?

When trying to pinpoint your language, pay attention to how *you* express love. We tend to express love in the way we wish to receive it. It's human nature to do for others what we would like done for us in return. When you are deliberately, consciously seeking to show your love for another person, does it involve spending quality time together or physically touching or giving a gift? If so, there's a good chance that's your primary love language.

It's harder to identify others' love languages. To figure it out, pay attention to how they express love to you and to others. When they want to do something kind for someone else, what form does it take? This may be an indicator of their primary love languages.

It's helpful to spend some time thinking about your love language and the love languages of your loved ones. However, there's no need to get obsessive. For one, Chapman believes we can be bilingual. Second, the biggest danger of the love languages is being totally blind to their existence and importance because of the misunderstandings and hurt that can result. If you've spent time reflecting thoughtfully, the blind spot isn't so blind anymore.

When Two People Don't Speak the Same Language

What happens when two people who love each other don't speak the same language? It might look something like this. Imagine Will and I have a free Saturday afternoon. I want to do something really nice for him to make him feel loved and appreciated, so I plan to mow the grass, mulch the flower beds, and make our yard look *amazing*. (If you spotted acts of service at work, kudos for paying attention. I hate yard work, and acts of service isn't really Will's love language, but work with me.)

But Will has different plans. He wants to brew two cups of coffee, get out that list of things we've been meaning to talk about, and take a long walk. (This plan has quality time written all over it.)

You can see the conflict brewing, right? It would be *so easy* for one—or both—of us to get our feelings hurt by dinnertime. I want to show him I love him by doing the pesky yard work, but Will just doesn't care all that much. He's not going to appreciate my efforts. Even worse, he's going to feel as though I prioritized yard work—which he knows I don't even like!—over spending time with him. (To his way of thinking, I would have done the opposite if I had wanted to show him I loved him.)

Speaking Your Child's Love Language

For a child to be emotionally healthy, they need to know, without a doubt, that they are loved. Without this assurance, they cannot feel safe and secure. This is where the love languages come in. While it's beneficial for a child to receive love in all five languages, their primary language identifies how they best understand a parent's love.

Chapman says it's impossible to discover a child's primary love language prior to age five—don't even try. During this stage, and at any stage when you're in doubt as to your child's primary love language, strive to speak all five languages fluently, expressing your love in myriad ways. (If you're not sure how to best demonstrate love or appreciation, this is not a bad strategy for any age or setting—shower your people with all five until you figure out which means the most to them.)

Here's a quick peek at what the love languages look like in action for children.

Words of Affirmation and the Child

Words are always a powerful way to communicate love. The emotional tanks of children whose primary love language is words of affirmation cannot stay full without receiving words of affirmation from their parents. Don't even think about saying you're just not expressive. For your child's emotional health, you need to learn how to use your words.

The right kind of praise is extremely important, and much has been written on this (apart from the love languages). To children, the volume you use and the manner in which you say something matter a great deal.

Especially in regard to children, it's important to remember the flip side of the love languages. Cutting words always have the potential to be detrimental, but they will be more so to a child whose primary love language is words of affirmation.

Children with this love language appreciate hearing "I love you," of course, but they also need a sincere thank-you for a job well done, a Post-it in their lunch box with a kind note written on it, or a phone call to say you're thinking of them.

Quality Time and the Child

Children with quality time as their primary love language crave their parents' undivided attention. They need to feel their presence is personally important to you.

I have one daughter who, more than my other kids, seeks quality time from the people she loves. She enjoys and invites one-on-one time by asking to read a story with me or taking a walk with my dad or running an errand with my husband. Her requests often include the key phrase "just you and me." As in, "Mom, can we have a tea party, just you and me?"

Giving your child quality time might mean playing a game together, going out for ice cream, or watching their soccer game. It may involve sitting on the living room rug playing trucks or having a competition to see who can make the biggest cannonball splash in the pool. It may mean regular family mealtimes or a special bedtime ritual. Other family rituals can be great, such as paddleboarding (something we do as a family on vacation) or hiking or eating pizza on Friday nights. In families with multiple children, it may mean making space for one-on-one time, whether it's just for a few minutes or for an afternoon out.

I know a family with twelve children, and the parents say it's difficult to get quality one-on-one time with each of their kids because there are so many of them. The dad once told me he *always* grabs just one child to bring along when he runs to the grocery store or the bank or the Home Depot, because they can have great one-on-one conversations in the car.

Gifts and the Child

The love language of gifts has little to do with money and everything to do with love. Children whose primary love language is receiving gifts get their emotional needs met when they receive physical, tangible expressions of love. These gifts are an important symbol to these children.

Keep in mind that there's a big difference between expressing love and spoiling a child. And if gift-giving is abused, children can recognize when they're receiving gifts not as expressions of love but as substitutes for love.

Children with this primary love language even appreciate the kinds of gifts that don't have to be bought—a postcard from your vacation spot, an interesting pebble you found on a walk, or a handwritten note or letter. These children especially value when you serve them food on a special plate, take extra effort to make a pretty snack, or pack something special just for them when you set off for that road trip or are even just out running errands for a long time.

Acts of Service and the Child

Parenting means serving. Parents do stuff for their kids all the time. They provide food, shelter, clothing—and are expected to do so. They cook, they clean, they run carpool, and they do laundry. Parenting babies and toddlers can feel like *nonstop* acts of service.

Understanding this love language gets complicated because so much of parenting *is* service. When it comes to the love language of service, we're talking about the kind of service that is a gift, given deliberately as a purposeful expression of love—not out of duty, necessity, or obligation. These acts of service aren't given because we have to, and they're definitely not for the purpose of behavior modification (as in, "Get an A on that test, and I'll take you out for ice cream").

Most children will be emotionally impacted by acts of service done freely out of love for them. But for children with this primary love language, these acts of service are how they most deeply *feel* loved. This means serving your kids when you don't have to and in a way that matters to your child. When I was in high school, I was overcome with the notion that I needed to make my bedroom more sophisticated. My parents not only let me repaint my room from pale blue to a deep brick red, but they also helped me choose the precise color. My mom drove me to the store to pick out a new grown-up comforter. I think she paid for it too, but what I most remember years later is the time and effort she put into helping me complete my special project.

If your child's primary love language is acts of service, you can also express your love by doting on them when they are sick, making them a special breakfast every once in a while, helping them get ready (without berating them!) when they oversleep, or helping them find their favorite teddy bear (or for older kids, their car keys).

Of course, doing your kid's laundry can be an act of service, but so can teaching them to do it themselves (especially if they're headed off to college soon) or showing them how to wash the car. You're teaching them essential life skills, which is both the job of a parent and an act of love, especially if you're doing it not just because you want to get them off your back but because you want them to be properly equipped for the real world.

Physical Touch and the Child

All children need to be touched—and often. This doesn't mean only "affectionate" touch—hugs, cuddles, and kisses. Throughout the childhood years, much physical touch comes through playing games: tickle fights, wrestling, high fives, fist bumps. Touch is especially important to kids who have this as their primary love language.

Incorporating physical touch into everyday life can be simple: a high five when you pass in the hallway and warm greetings and goodbyes, including a hug, a kiss, or just a pat on the shoulder. Group hugs among family members are a good way to incorporate physical touch and something that teenagers may not be as resistant to. At my house, we smush our kids into group hugs, making "Silas sandwiches" or "Sarah tacos." They'll probably reach an age when they're not okay with this anymore, but we're not there yet.

Speaking the Languages of Appreciation outside the Home

The love languages aren't confined to family life.

Everyone wants to feel as though the work they do matters, whether it's the kind of work that builds a career, brings home a paycheck, involves volunteering, or means running errands on a Tuesday afternoon. And we feel like what we do matters when other people appreciate it—and us. We need to feel appreciation to enjoy our work, to give it our best effort, and to keep it up for the long term.

But what makes one person feel appreciated might not make another person feel the same way. We tend not to hear or notice this appreciation unless it's expressed in a way we can truly understand.

Because talking about love languages at your tech company could be weird or uncomfortable, in work settings, Chapman calls the love languages the "languages of appreciation."[3] At work, we all need to know intellectually that we're appreciated— and we also need to feel it. It's not just about feeling warm and fuzzy; feeling appreciated boosts job satisfaction and improves the overall quality of relationships in the workplace and between coworkers. Reflecting on these languages helps us to be self-aware, proactive, and kind. Even if nobody else understands the languages of appreciation you're trying to speak, your own experience will improve as you shift your focus toward appreciation for what others are doing well.

Being sensitive to the languages of others can be a huge help in the work we're doing, whether that work is paid, in a committee meeting, or in a neighborhood. On garbage day, my retired neighbor faithfully drags the garbage cans from the curb back to where they belong for all the parents of young children on our street. That's appreciation in action.

Years ago, I supervised someone who was in the midst of a personal crisis. She was exhausted and distracted, and her work was suffering. We were reviewing yet another project she'd done that was rife with critical errors when she stopped me and said she had an odd request. "I know I'm not doing great work right now, and it's killing me," she said. "But could you please tell me when I actually do something well? I know it sounds strange—especially now—but it's really important to me."

Her language of appreciation was words of encouragement, so I immediately shifted my focus to what she was doing correctly and started telling her whenever I spotted her doing something well. Since that time, I've made it a habit to notice and appreciate—out loud—what the people I work with are doing correctly. Whether their primary love language is words of affirmation doesn't matter. It certainly can't hurt to affirm their good work, and it's great for *my* outlook to focus on the positive instead of only calling out people for messing up.

If your relationships could stand to be better, then take it on yourself to make the first step, if only for your own sake. It's a fact of life that people tend to get what they give. Start experimenting with expressing appreciation to others in various ways—using all five languages—and see what happens. Which language do the various individuals around you respond to best? You won't know until you try.

Specific Help for *How* to Love

Our old house was easy to find, just one block off a major street. If I told you to get off the highway, find my street, and turn right, those directions would be accurate. But if you were coming to that house, those aren't the directions I would give you.

My directions would go more like this: Stay in the left lane as you exit the highway, headed north. You'll pass a Home Depot, then a church as you enter a residential area. When you pass another church, slow down—you're getting close, three or so more blocks. The street sign is hard to see because the neighbor's tree hangs down low; that's where you hang a right. If you reach the stoplight (the one with yet another church on the corner), you've gone too far. Your GPS will say our house is in the middle of the block; your GPS is wrong. We're the last house on the left—stone with a white fence.

I'd tell you all this because I would want you to get to the right place, and even though the simpler directions seem straightforward, I am keenly aware of all the ways people have screwed up those directions in the past. They didn't realize they had headed south instead of north; they turned too early because they felt like they'd gone far enough; they turned too late because they couldn't see the sign. I have had people call me from my neighbor's driveway down the block because their GPS said they had arrived, but they didn't see my dog in the yard. There are many ways to go wrong.

Similarly, the love languages provide us with detailed information about how to show love. Plenty of people, never having heard of the love languages, navigate by simple directions, such as "show your love to the people you care about." That seems straightforward enough, but experience has shown there are plenty of ways to screw that up. The detailed directions tell you more about the landscape you're moving through. You know what to expect. You know what trouble spots to watch out for. And you know how to tell if you've gotten off course *before* anything disastrous happens.

I give my friends careful directions to my house to spare them a little frustration. Because getting off course is no fun, not even if you're just stopping by for coffee. With a little extra information, they make it to the right place almost every time. And if a few extra directions—in the form of the love languages—can help me understand how to help the people I love *feel* my love for them, then I say bring it on! It's easy to screw up seemingly simple things—in my neighborhood or in my relationships—and I'll take all the help I can get.

5

You're Not Crazy, You're Just Not Me

keirsey's temperaments

A few years ago, I was concerned about one of my kids. For the purposes of this story, this kid's name is Bronte. Because I'm sure I embarrass my kids enough already without putting their names in books, I turned to a random baby name generator online,[1] and Bronte's what I got. I appreciate its literary heritage, plus—according to this baby-naming website—it's gender neutral, though it's more commonly used for girls. So Bronte it is.

Bronte was born cautious. She wants advance notice for everything. If we're going to the beach in August, she wants to know in January. She wants to know on Sunday what we're having for dinner Friday night. She doesn't love the idea of taking a new way home from Grandma's house. I worried about these sorts of behaviors, wondering if my child was too rigid or inflexible, particularly when it came to schoolwork and organizing the house and daily routines. I considered scheduling a checkup with our family therapist to probe the behaviors I was seeing because I couldn't make sense of them.

It's no wonder I couldn't understand her behaviors; Bronte and I often feel like opposites. My child embraces routine; I fight it. When I implement structure, I do so reluctantly. I don't like to make plans too far in advance. I enjoy improvising in the kitchen.

When I was a new mom, I read something in a parenting book that's haunted me ever since. The author said something to the effect that "goodness of fit" between parent and child is an essential factor for the success of that relationship, yet it's difficult to control. Getting a good match is pretty much the luck of the draw.

I was concerned that when it came to Bronte and me, I was dealing with a less-than-ideal match. I considered consulting a professional because I needed a confidence boost. I wanted someone outside the situation to verify that I was nurturing this important relationship well. I wanted to hear that I wasn't screwing up my kid. I wanted to learn what I could do to help ease any anxiety Bronte might have and to ensure I wasn't fueling it.

My husband calmed me down. He said, "You don't completely understand Bronte. I don't completely understand her, either. But I think she's okay. I just don't think she's like you. Or me."

I wanted him to be right, but I wasn't sure.

Not long after, I happened to pick up *Please Understand Me II* by clinical psychologist David Keirsey, the book that led to the *aha!* moment I write about in chapter 1. The book explains complicated personality concepts in an accessible way, especially as they relate to personal relationships. Keirsey outlines four basic temperaments—four distinct, foundational combinations of characteristic attitudes, values, and talents. Each one of us can be sorted into one of these four temperaments. Keirsey focuses on how different types interact with one another, for good and for ill. He identifies what's likely to cause conflict and how to manage those issues. He describes how different types are apt to relate as spouses and as parent and child. He also explains how each type is likely to complement another and how they're likely to drive one another crazy.

I flipped straight to the chapter on parenting and found myself nodding along as I started reading. It was clear Bronte is a little "Guardian" type, as Keirsey calls it, an SJ type (Sensing + Judging, but if that makes no sense to you, that's fine; we'll talk all about it in the next chapter) who has a security-seeking personality, builds her self-esteem on her dependability, and is prone to guilt. This kind of person responds happily to well-established, clearly defined routines that bring her predictability.

I know *my* Guardian did.

I recognized myself in the book's pages too. I resonated with the description of the "Idealist" type, an NF (Intuition + Feeling) type. Idealists value harmony and hate conflict. They love to have deep, meaningful relationships with a small circle of people, which can include their children. In stark contrast to Guardians, Idealists are good with innovative ideas and spontaneous plans.

The paradigm was eye-opening. Guardians seek security, uphold tradition, and protect the status quo. But Idealists seek possibilities, imagine alternative futures, and love to ask, "What if?" These fundamentally different viewpoints affect everything from the way you make a grocery list to the way you schedule your day to the way you choose your career. It's no wonder Bronte and I were frustrating each other.

Unfortunately, all parents project themselves onto their children to one degree or another, and we expect them to resemble us more than we ought. It's a hazard of being human, and of being the authority figure in that particular relationship. It's especially easy for Idealists to do this because this type sees possibility and potential *everywhere*. Because of their intense focus on personal growth—their own and that of others—Idealists are especially apt to try to make over their children in their own image.

Even though I didn't realize that's what I was doing, I was still doing it. As I paid closer attention to my interactions regarding my child, I realized where I was going wrong. I told Bronte "Just don't worry about it" when she asked at 8:00 a.m. what was for dinner that night or when she wanted to plan ahead for the weekend on Monday or in a hundred other situations where she wanted structure and I was reluctant to provide it. I didn't operate that way, so why should she? (I know, I know.)

I was lucky to stumble on this personality framework and on its description of the Guardian-Idealist parent-child matchup, which captured my own relationship with my child with uncanny accuracy. My behavior wasn't healthy, but it was unhealthy in a very normal way. Once I could see what was actually happening between us, we could move past it. And that could happen almost immediately.

Keirsey writes that for this pairing to work, the Idealist needs to understand that their little Guardian is a "both-feet-on-the-ground little person who is unusually concerned about responsibility, security, authority, and belonging, but who displays little of [the Idealist's] romanticism or enthusiasm."[2] In other words, my child was acting exactly like herself, and not like me. I was projecting my own temperament onto her, but she already had her own. Bronte didn't need fixing. She was growing into the person *she* was born to be. I could encourage her to be who she was—even help her become a better version of herself—but I shouldn't try to change her into someone she wasn't. I especially shouldn't try to change her into someone like me.

The more I paid attention to the way we interacted, the clearer it became that the real thing that needed fixing was my point of view. I needed to accept my child for who she was. While I'll admit this was frustrating at times (I need to take into account someone's need for structure for the rest of my parenting days?), it was tremendously freeing.

What You Need to Know about Keirsey's Temperaments

The idea that there are four basic temperaments found in human personality has ancient roots. Some scholars believe the first mention of the temperaments can be found in the Old Testament book of Ezekiel, thousands of years before Christ. In chapter 1, Ezekiel has a vision (which might be familiar to anyone who sang "Ezekiel Saw the Wheel" as a child) in which he sees four living creatures in the fire—a lion, an ox, a man, and an eagle, each with a human face. Some scholars believe these four faces are references to the temperaments.

Hippocrates is often credited with introducing the four temperaments, as he incorporated the four "humors" into his medical theories in 400 BC. He believed each individual's personality and behavior were influenced by these four humors, or bodily fluids: blood, yellow bile, black bile, and phlegm.[3] One's dominant humor most influenced their behavior.

Ancient literature and culture are steeped in the temperaments, as we find references to the humors in the writings of Aristotle, Chaucer, Montaigne, Johnson, Hume, Rousseau, Tolstoy, Lawrence . . . and the list goes on and on. In *The Republic* from 340 BC, Plato writes of "four kinds of men," each with different strengths, roles, and ways of thinking. Shakespeare demonstrated a great familiarity with the ancient temperaments. Lady Macbeth was a powerful choleric, Sir John Falstaff a phlegmatic, Viola a sanguine heroine.

One of Shakespeare's most famous characters—and perhaps the most famous melancholic in all of literature—is Hamlet. At the play's opening, Hamlet's mother—noticing his darkening disposition—impels him, "Good Hamlet, cast thy nighted color off."[4] Hamlet suffers from a serious excess of melancholy (also evidenced by Shakespeare's many references to "black bile" in a time when any excessive imbalance was a sign of poor health). As the play progresses, Hamlet descends deeper and deeper into grief, then madness, until he eventually destroys himself and those around him. To Shakespeare's original audience, the implications of his melancholy were clear: this was a tragedy.

Throughout history, these temperaments have been referred to in various ways: blood, yellow bile, black bile, phlegm. Sanguine, choleric, melancholy, phlegmatic. Air, fire, earth, water. Artisan, Guardian, Idealist, Rational.

David Keirsey developed his temperament framework in the 1950s and codified his theories into a tool known as the Keirsey Temperament Sorter II. I encountered Keirsey's temperament theory years after I first discovered the Myers-Briggs Type Indicator but understood it years sooner. This is no surprise, since Keirsey's theory has fewer moving pieces, which makes it much easier for a layperson—and a newbie at that—to grasp.

Despite their differences, Keirsey and the MBTI do overlap, and understanding Keirsey is a great foundation if you want to understand the more complex (and slightly different) Myers-Briggs Type Indicator. While there are sixteen MBTI types, Keirsey's framework has only four core temperaments. Keirsey's limited list of temperaments makes correctly identifying your own type—and the types of the people you love—doable.

Determining your temperament is straightforward, although that doesn't necessarily mean it's easy.

Two Factors that Determine Temperament

Under Keirsey's framework, two factors determine temperament: how we use words (what we say) and how we use tools (what we do). According to Keirsey, all of us lean toward being concrete or abstract in our word usage and are either cooperative or utilitarian in our tool usage.

The way these two factors interact is plotted on a two-by-two matrix, which indicates how the four temperaments are likely to act and use language. (I don't want to lose you here. This is really fun, but it is like learning a new language. Thankfully, it's a simple—and useful—one.)

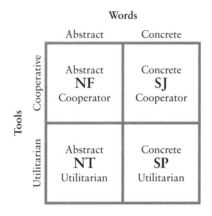

Those with concrete word usage—Guardians (SJ) and Artisans (SP)—are most concerned with things that can be seen, touched, and handled. They are literal, factual, and detailed in their communication. They focus on—and verbalize—what is.

In contrast, those who are abstract in word usage—Idealists (NF) and Rationalists (NT)—don't need to anchor their communication in the touchable and tangible, preferring instead to deal in the realm of ideas, possibilities, and the imagination. They focus on—and verbalize—what's possible. These people are in their element when they theorize, philosophize, and hypothesize. They love metaphors and superlatives.

The concept of tool usage is harder to grasp. To Keirsey, a tool is anything that can be used to effect action. An espresso machine is a tool, but so is a highway or a house or the Democratic Party or the PTA. A tool is something, anything, that gets things done.

There are two basic approaches to tool usage: utilitarian and cooperative. Those with a utilitarian approach to tool usage want to do whatever works. They don't care if it's traditional, socially acceptable, or aesthetically pleasing, as long as it gets the job done. Those with a cooperative approach to tool usage want to do what's right. They value cooperation and social conventions, so much so that they prioritize these things over effectiveness.

The combination of these two traits—word usage + tool usage—produces four possible temperaments. Some people are able to immediately recognize whether their communication is concrete or abstract and whether their actions are utilitarian or cooperative. Others need to read more descriptions of how the combination of these two factors practically plays out in everyday life. (Keirsey's official Keirsey Temperament Sorter II is in his book *Please Understand Me II* or is available free online.)[5]

The following descriptions will help you further understand the types.

What Each Temperament Is Like

The four temperaments provide a foundational understanding of four different types of people.

It's fascinating to discover how the types flesh out and how they interact with one another. As you read the descriptions of the four temperaments, it's easy to see how misunderstandings could so easily erupt between different types due to nothing more than each person's fundamentally different way of seeing the world. In the abstract, it's clear that the world needs all four types, but in the day to day, the variety in personalities causes all kinds of conflict when we don't understand why someone else doesn't see things our way.

Artisans (SPs)[6]

Words: concrete

Tools: utilitarian

Artisans make up a significant percentage of the population (30–35 percent).[7] They're artistic, adaptable, and easygoing. They have a real talent for enjoying life because they live in the moment and are thoroughly grounded in the real world. They accept reality for what it *is* instead of daydreaming about what it *could be*. They're fun-loving, open-minded, and tolerant. They're right-brained makers and creators.

Artisans are great with machines and tools of all sorts. They have a strong aesthetic sense, but more than just appreciating beauty, they want to *create*, whether they're making works of art or more practical things.

More than any other temperament, Artisans love excitement and hate being bored. They prefer variety over the familiar. Artisans are people of decisive action—they're impulsive. They think quickly on their feet. They're confident, and they trust their instincts.

They will try anything once and are fans of trial and error, which leads to some great experiments with smashing results. Artisans are often innovators, putting their tactical intellect to good use.

Keirsey sums up Artisans by saying, "Artisans make playful mates, creative parents, and troubleshooting leaders."[8]

Harry Potter is a good example of an Artisan in action. Harry is passionate about the things that matter to him. He has good instincts about people. He's well-liked by most. He can be reckless and impulsive, living very much in the moment, and he'd always rather be chasing an adventure than tidying up the details, which he happily leaves to Hermione. Luckily for the reader, Harry's madcap adventures make for great reading. (For those of you who are familiar with the Myers-Briggs Type Indicator, the corresponding types are ESTP, ISFP, ISTP, ESFP.)

Guardians (SJs)

Words: concrete

Tools: cooperative

Guardians comprise 40–45 percent of the population,[9] outnumbering all other temperaments. Sensible and judicious, Guardians are the sort we think of as the pillars of society. These reliable, dependable, and consistent types uphold (or "stand guard over") the status quo: they care deeply about protocol and tradition. They are creatures of habit who love their routines. Guardians are intensely logical, innately modest, and known for their common sense. They're focused on the present—on what *is*—and not on what *could be*.

Guardians are straightforward in their speech and precise in the way they describe what's happening. They love facts and are good at remembering details: names, birthdays, anniversaries, social events. This makes them good at administration, seeing that everything is in its proper place.

They are hard workers with a strong work ethic. Give Guardians a job to do and you can count on them to do it. Guardians take care of many of the world's "thankless jobs" and often volunteer in their communities and churches.

In relationships, they're a stable influence and make "loyal mates, responsible parents, and steadying leaders."[10]

Guardians seek responsibility and are apt to be military officers, CEOs, and judges. They often study business, law, and other practical fields. According to Keirsey, nearly half of the US presidents have been Guardians.[11]

Marilla Cuthbert in *Anne of Green Gables* provides a wonderful example of a Guardian in action. Matthew and Marilla Cuthbert think they're adopting an orphan boy to help on the farm, but the neighbor sent to fetch the child from the orphanage shows up with Anne instead. The only reason Marilla doesn't send the poor girl straight back is that keeping her seemed "a sort of duty."[12] Marilla greatly respects tradition, propriety, and the status quo. She's a hard worker and a creature of habit. In Anne's young life, Marilla is a responsible and steadying influence. Many of the story's funny moments come from the stark juxtaposition of Marilla's Guardian temperament with Anne's Idealist one, as in the following exchange:

> Anne: "Marilla, I dreamt last night that I arrived at the ball in puffed sleeves and everyone was overcome by my regal . . ."
> Marilla: "Regal, my eye. You're dripping dirty, greasy water all over my clean floor!"[13]

(The corresponding MBTI types are ESTJ, ISTJ, ISFJ, ESFJ.)

Idealists (NFs)

Words: abstract

Tools: cooperative

Keirsey estimates Idealists make up 15–20 percent of the population.[14] Insightful, imaginative, and empathetic, Idealists care deeply about finding meaning and significance in the world, particularly in their relationships. They're great idea people, interested in possibilities and unseen potential, and they are able to draw connections between seemingly unrelated ideas. As opposed to Artisans and Guardians, who focus on what *is*, Idealists are focused on what *could be*.

Idealists adore metaphors and have a penchant for hyperbole. They are extremely good at putting themselves in someone else's shoes. They are sensitive to nuance and good readers of body language and facial expression. They trust their intuition, their first impressions, and their feelings. As a group, they're generally positive, highly emotional, and prone to wishful thinking.

Idealists believe everyone is unique and special in their own way. It's true that Idealists probably see themselves as special snowflakes, but the truth is they see *you* as one too. This is why out of all the temperaments, Idealists are most likely to go gaga over personality typing of any sort. They are fascinated by identity and devoted to pursuing, identifying, and understanding their own. They need to understand themselves and strive to understand others as well.

In relationships, Idealists make "intense mates, nurturing parents, and inspirational leaders."[15]

Idealists excel at sharing ideas through words and tend to be speakers, writers, teachers, and communicators. You'll find Idealists in mental health services, missionary work, and ministry.

Kathleen Kelly in *You've Got Mail* shows us what an Idealist could look like in action.[16] She is idealistic, hopeful, and personally attentive to the people in her life—both her friends and her customers. Despite trying to adopt Joe Fox's mantra—"It's not personal, it's business"—Kathleen cannot help but be personal in her relationships. She is sure her store will pull through even when the balance sheets indicate it won't. When she breaks up with Frank, she tells him there isn't someone else, but there is the "dream of someone." She is optimistic, imaginative, and intent on finding meaning in her life and her work. These are all strong Idealist tendencies.

(The corresponding MBTI types are ENFJ, INFP, INFJ, ENFP.)

Rationals (NTs)

Words: abstract

Tools: utilitarian

Rationals focus on the imaginable as opposed to the concrete, what *could be* instead of what *is*. Keirsey's guess is that they make up no more than 5–6 percent of the population,[17] yet they fill a valuable role. These intelligent, logical, and contemplative types are excellent at envisioning solutions to problems real, imagined, or hypothetical. They're experimental, open-minded, and flexible and don't care one bit about social politics, political correctness, or tradition.

Rationals have zero interest in trivial matters and therefore aren't interested in small talk. They're not comfortable with bragging or self-promotion. They also don't waste words; Rationals rarely repeat themselves and take pains never to state the obvious, assuming that what is obvious to them is obvious to everyone. They care deeply about defining things precisely and run into trouble when others perceive this as being nitpicky.

These curious and analytical types love to build theories and solve problems. They care about assembling coherent arguments and are driven to understand how things work so they can figure out how to make them work better. They care about being efficient, which means they are always on the lookout for inefficiencies in the system. They are skeptical and always searching for errors in order to fix them (if only in their minds). Rationals are pragmatic to the core—utilitarian about going after what they want. They appear cool, calm, and collected, making them prone to being mistaken as cold and distant. According to Keirsey, "Rationals make reasonable mates, individualizing parents, and strategic leaders."[18]

Fitzwilliam Darcy, the gentleman in *Pride and Prejudice* with an income of more than ten thousand British pounds a year, is a wonderful example of a Rational in action.[19] He hates small talk, is unsurprisingly terrible at it, and offends everyone with his awkward manner at the first Netherfield ball. He's pragmatic to the core, as evidenced by his advice to Bingley about Jane's disinterest, and utilitarian about going after what he wants, whether it's securing Elizabeth for himself or persuading Wickham to marry Lydia, despite being personally repulsed by the match. His character changes throughout the novel, to be sure, but he's eventually able to persuade Elizabeth to marry him because she becomes acquainted with what's going on beneath the surface of his cool, calm, and collected demeanor.

(The corresponding MBTI types are ENTJ, INTP, INTJ, ENTP.)

Putting This Information to Work in Your Own Life

Which of the four temperaments best describes *you*? Many people can confidently type themselves after reading through the short descriptions in this chapter. But if you are not sure or just want to confirm your answer, I recommend using Keirsey's Temperament Sorter II.

Get Comfortable with the Four Temperaments

If you want to put this information to work in your own life—and I certainly hope you do—spend some time familiarizing yourself with the temperament descriptions. Many people have experiences similar to my own, meaning they immediately recognize they're an Idealist, their child is a Guardian, they're married to a Rational, or their boss is an Artisan. Let it soak in that, yeah, these people are different from you, and they're supposed to be.

When I start talking about temperament with people, sometimes they'll ask, "But which temperament is *best*?" My answer is always, "Best for what?"

Each temperament has certain characteristics; we cannot be all things to all people. Each temperament has great strengths, but no one temperament has every possible strength. We can't be traditional *and* cutting-edge, detail-oriented *and* big-picture-oriented, staid *and* spontaneous.

Illustrating delicate points is often easier using fictional characters, so let me pull an example from a wonderful novel. In Chitra Banerjee Divakaruni's *Before We Visit the Goddess*, a relationship begins to dissolve because, after many years together, a man begins to feel that his partner is boring—predictable, traditional, never wanting to try new things. But what the man doesn't perceive—but the author wants the reader to see—is that his partner is also dependable, trustworthy, and loyal, and this man adores his partner because of these very traits. Divakaruni guides the reader to see what her character cannot: this character wouldn't want to forgo the admirable traits, and it's highly unlikely—if not downright impossible—for one individual to be both risk-seeking *and* steady or bubbly *and* serious.

Reality check: no one individual can meet *all* our needs. It's like wanting your spouse to be tall, except on the days you'd rather they be short.

No Ordinary People

The thing to realize about understanding temperament is that it changes more than your perception of one particular facet of your personality, or your relationship. As you become more aware of the amazing variety of people and experiences, your worldview changes, making you more humble, more open, more aware of the possibilities in each person you encounter. I'm reminded of C. S. Lewis's marvelous essay *The Weight of Glory*. He writes, "There are no ordinary people. You have never talked to a mere mortal." In light of Lewis's eternal view of life after death—heaven and hell—he explains, "All day long we are, in some degree helping each other to one or the other of these destinations. It is in the light of these overwhelming possibilities, it is with the awe and the circumspection proper to them, that we should conduct all of our dealings with one another, all friendships, all love, all play, all politics."[20]

In our everyday lives, we encounter people who aren't like us *all the time*. Sometimes our poor little brains don't know how to handle these differences, and we behave badly. Instead of being grateful that we live in a world that contains artists and attorneys and musicians and managers and teachers and taxi drivers and chefs and people who do any number of things, we encounter these people and freak out because *they're not like us*. Perhaps we even *wish* they were more like us. Thinking this way is a totally normal impulse—but be careful what you wish for.

When You Wish Someone Were More like You

It's human nature to make a fleeting wish for someone to be more like you. However, when you try to make that person *become* more like you—intentionally or unintentionally—well, Keirsey calls that a "Pygmalion project," and you do not want to be involved in one in any way, shape, or form. Although, if I had to bet, I'd say you probably have been involved in one in some way or another. Most of us have.

The phrase "Pygmalion project" comes from the Greek figure Pygmalion, who is best known from his appearance in Ovid's poem "Metamorphoses." In the poem, Pygmalion is a sculptor who carves his perfect woman out of ivory and then falls in love with her. When Aphrodite grants his wish to bring the sculpture to life, he marries her.

The 1964 Audrey Hepburn film *My Fair Lady* shows a Pygmalion project in action. In fact, the film was originally called *Pygmalion*. Hepburn plays Eliza Doolittle, a young working-class flower seller with a thick Cockney accent. Rex Harrison plays arrogant phonetics scholar Henry Higgins, who makes a bet of sorts that he can "transform" the roughest raw material—in this case, Eliza Doolittle—and pass her off as a duchess at a royal ball by training her to speak differently. His experiment is a success. Higgins receives heaps of praise, while Eliza receives none—and, whoa, did she *hate* being treated as an experiment.

We may watch Higgins on screen and think, *I would never do that*. But it's easy to take on our own Pygmalion project, attempting to similarly sculpt a loved one into our ideal image (which often looks like *our* image) instead of accepting them for who they are. Just flip back to the beginning of this chapter and you'll see what I mean.

It is especially easy for parents to play Pygmalion with their children, without even realizing they are doing it. We want to raise our children "right," except our natural understanding of what this means may be right for us but not right for them. And parents aren't the only ones who make this mistake.

While Idealists are the most apt of the types to undertake a Pygmalion project, we all make these kinds of mistakes—especially when we don't perceive the wide and beautiful variety of human temperaments. Thankfully, if we know there are sharp curves ahead, then we can be better prepared when we take the wheel.

I once caught a glimpse of a Pygmalion project in action in my own backyard—although this time I wasn't the instigator. My husband and I were hosting friends for dinner, a couple we knew casually from a class we were teaching at church. We'd had plenty of conversations with them before but never in this intimate a setting. We didn't know the couple, who had just celebrated their first wedding anniversary, that well, but we liked them a lot.

As we all sat around the table in our backyard by the grill, a conversational pattern became increasingly and painfully obvious. It went something like this.

Wife: We were in the Dominican Republican four
years ago—
Husband: It was five years and four months ago.
Wife: Well, when we were in the Dominican Republic
and we had those really great fried bananas—
Husband: They weren't bananas. They were plantains.
Wife: And we were with our friends Mark and
Hayley—
Husband: But Hayley didn't come until later . . .

He fact-checked everything she said in real time and corrected every single unimportant detail that came out of her mouth. It was second nature to him but *exhausting* to us.

I found a gentle way to ask the husband about it there at the table (Idealist that I am, who values preserving harmony above all). I was embarrassed for the both of them—her for being corrected and him for being rude. I tried to gently say so. "I'd just like to hear the story!" I said.

"Yeah, but I always help her get the details right," he said. "*Everyone* wants to get the details right!"

That is the belief of a Guardian type who is detailed, factual, and logical and who loves facts and cares about precision.

His wife was not a Guardian.

And thereafter followed an enlightening conversation. The non-Guardians of the world will not be surprised to hear that the wife did not enjoy having her husband, the self-appointed Fact Police, correct her every factual slip in conversation both between themselves and in front of others. He thought he was trying to help her be a better person, but, really, he was trying to make her more like him. He was doing it out of love, but it didn't seem loving to his wife. Months later, my friend—the wife in this couple—called me to say that once they understood the dynamics at play, they were able to adjust accordingly, and the adjustment made *both* of them happier. Will and I were happier too because their conversations no longer wore us out!

The Point: Improved Empathy

The point of the four temperaments isn't to put people in boxes or to definitively describe all human behavior. The point is to get us out of the boxes we're trapped in by helping us grasp the insights we need for improved empathy through better understanding. When we understand what's happening with regard to people's varying personalities, we can appreciate their differences—and the fundamental need for those differences—instead of doing what we usually do, which is get all crazy about them.

Instead of trying to force someone else into a box they don't belong in or lamenting why we can't be more like somebody else, we can learn to understand the different points of view we all bring to the table. When we better comprehend our differences, we can appreciate them for what they are—even if that's no guarantee they won't drive us bonkers every once in a while. It's still important to understand what's going on—and why.

Not a Roll of the Dice

When it comes to temperament, the world needs all four types. We wouldn't want to be without Artisans, Guardians, Idealists, or Rationals. And all four types can and do go together in work, play, love, or whatever—although each pairing has its own strengths and perils. According to Keirsey's framework, or any of the others in this book, two reasonably well-adjusted people can build a relationship that works well for them, no matter their temperaments. The key is to understand the factors at play, appreciate each person's strengths and weaknesses, and enter the relationship with realistic expectations.

I've come to believe that old parenting book I mentioned earlier was wrong. I no longer believe "goodness of fit" is a roll of the dice. A good match isn't something you're given; it's something you make. Any combination can be a good fit if you accept the other person for who they are and lovingly support them in becoming the best person they can be.

Remember that temperament only begins to describe who we are. Understanding and appreciating one another seem easy enough, of course, but can be brutal in actual practice. It's tough to learn to see things from someone else's point of view. While it is work to learn about and better communicate with another person, it's the best kind of work. And in my experience, understanding Keirsey's four temperaments has made it significantly easier.

6

Type Talk

the myers-briggs type indicator

A few years ago, my family decided to try a new vacation spot. Will and I thought about visiting any number of cities and small towns within three hundred miles of home. Once we narrowed it down to the shores of Lake Michigan, I was in charge of choosing the spot and booking a place to stay.

For months in advance, I browsed travel sites. I quizzed family members and Facebook friends. I pored over houses for rent on the internet. And finally, three days before we left home, I decided which little town we would visit and rented a house for our stay.

When I told a friend that I'd finally nailed down our plans, she said, "If we ever go on vacation together, I'm making the plans. I can't handle spontaneous people being in charge!"

I must have looked at her like she was crazy, because she quickly explained: "Don't get me wrong—I love my spontaneous friends! It's just that I freak out when things are left openended until the last minute. I can't believe it doesn't bother you."

Was she calling *me* spontaneous? Until that moment, I had always thought of myself as a planner. When I was in high school, I read every page of every college pamphlet I received—from at least two hundred schools. When I was in college, I loved sitting down with the course catalogs and mapping out my future. I put together course plans—for my freshman year straight through graduation—mapping out exactly what potential paths might look like, how many classes I'd be able to sample, and how many majors I'd be able to squeeze in.

Did you catch the key word in that last sentence? It's *potential*.

I love dreaming up future possibilities, examining situations and plans from every conceivable angle, and test-driving potential life paths in my head. I thought that meant I was a natural planner. And by "natural," I mean I thought I was someone who was good at and enjoyed planning. However, my friend's comment made me realize I was getting myself wrong—again. I'm much better at possibilities than plans.

With that friend's small remark, a few things clicked into place for me. Before that day, I had still been debating whether I was a J (for decisive Judging types) or a P (for open-ended Perceiving types) for my Myers-Briggs type (P, definitely P). I realized why I had had such a difficult time managing my calendar and why it had been that way for years. I also realized my spontaneous ways, while fine in and of themselves, were quite possibly stressing out my more methodical friends.

This was all so obvious I couldn't believe I hadn't seen it before. Yet there it was.

Once I knew I was definitely a P, I could start accounting for this preference in everything I did, from the way I planned my meetings to how I arranged my kids' playdates to how I booked my vacations. But not until then.

What You Need to Know about the MBTI

The Myers-Briggs Type Indicator is a personality inventory originally developed by Katharine C. Briggs and her daughter, Isabel Briggs Myers, nearly one hundred years ago. The two women greatly admired the work and psychological theories of Carl Jung but found them inaccessible to the general public and not particularly useful for everyday life. So they created an assessment tool. This was during World War II, and their goal was to help women who were entering the workforce for the first time because of the war effort identify the jobs for which they'd be best suited and the roles in which they'd be most effective.[1] Interestingly, that's how it's often still used today.

You'll recognize some of the letters in the MBTI from Keirsey's temperaments. While Keirsey's temperaments each combine two traits, the sixteen MBTI types signify four pairs of preferences, allowing for a more detailed understanding of each personality type.

The title Briggs and Myers gave one of their books, *Gifts Differing: Understanding Personality Type*, explains their mindset. The title comes from Romans 12:6 in the King James Version of the Bible, which says that we all have "gifts differing according to the grace that is given to us." And as you might expect, a fundamental belief of the MBTI system is that while certain types naturally have certain proclivities, there are no "good" types or "bad" types. All types are equal, and each type brings something important and necessary to the metaphorical table.

Like Keirsey's temperaments, the MBTI assessment shows how people's behaviors differ largely because they see the world through different lenses, although, with its sixteen types, the MBTI is able to do this on a more granular level. Every individual has been given different gifts and has a different viewpoint. Many conflicts are rooted in these differing worldviews, and the assessment helps people understand those differences.

The most common reaction people have to seeing their MBTI type is, "Oh, that explains so much!" Understanding your MBTI type can help you understand how to care for yourself and how to better relate to the people around you. It's similar to being given the owner's manual for a certain model of car—your preferred model.

What All Those Letters Really Mean

The MBTI is based on eight psychological preferences, which are broken down into four opposing pairs we'll call dichotomies. These four dichotomies generate sixteen possible combinations.

The four dichotomies are as follows:

- Introversion/Extraversion
- Intuition[2]/Sensing
- Thinking/Feeling
- Judging/Perceiving

As always, when determining personality type, it's critical to remember that we're all a little bit of everything. Each of us has all eight qualities in our mental tool belt. We are all introverted and extroverted, intuitive and sensing, and so forth.

The dichotomies simply capture the mental process in every pair that each of us is more inclined toward.

Let's examine the four dichotomies in more detail. To understand the MBTI inventory, it's essential that you understand the vocabulary of the indicator's framework.

Introversion/Extraversion (I/E)

The first set of preferences is Introversion and Extraversion. This preference explains the way one prefers to engage with the world. Do they prefer to turn their attention toward the external world or introspectively toward the world within them?

For Introverts, the inner world—the world of ideas—is what they think of as the real world. It's where the real action is and where they naturally prefer to spend their time. Interacting with ideas in their own heads is natural and effortless.

For Extroverts, the real world is external. The real action happens outside themselves, with other people and input. It's where they naturally prefer to spend their time and where they feel most at home.

Some describe this preference as being about energy management—whether a person is an Introvert or an Extrovert depends on where they focus their attention and how they get their energy. Do they feel energized after spending time alone or after spending time with others?

Anywhere from 30–50 percent of the population is introverted; the remainder of the population is extroverted.

Intuition/Sensing (N/S)

The second set of preferences is Intuition and Sensing. (Because Introversion is represented by an I, Intuition is represented

119

by an N.) This doesn't reference whether a person is thoughtful, or sensual; instead, it identifies how a person prefers to take in information from the world around them. Do they pay more attention to information taken in through their five senses, or do they focus instead on the underlying meaning of what they observe—the patterns and potentials of that information?

Intuitives naturally focus on the big picture, read between the lines, make connections from seemingly disconnected ideas, and see potentials and possibilities. They're drawn to what's going on beneath the surface and focus their attention on what *could be*. Sensors focus on observable facts: what they see, hear, smell, touch, and taste. They focus their attention on what *is*.

Sensors greatly outnumber Intuitives: 70–75 percent of the population identify as Sensing types, with females slightly outnumbering males.[3]

Thinking/Feeling (T/F)

The third set of preferences is Thinking and Feeling. These don't have anything to do with being thoughtful, intelligent, or emotional, whether a person's heart is cold or warm. Instead, they describe a person's natural decision-making process. Thinkers and Feelers naturally use different kinds of information when making decisions.

When making decisions, Thinkers are analytical, logical, and consistent; they rely on their reason as they search for fundamental truths and underlying principles. Because they are task-oriented and impartial, they are easily perceived as uncaring.

Feelers, however, are always evaluating how a decision will affect the people involved. They make decisions with their hearts and are often perceived as warm, caring, and compassionate.

They are tactful and likely to consider others' points of view, and they strive to maintain harmony with their decisions. While Feelers slightly outnumber Thinkers in the general population (at about 55–60 percent), 65–75 percent of women are Feelers.[4]

Judging/Perceiving (J/P)

The final set of preferences is Judging and Perceiving. This dichotomy has been called the lifestyle preference or the preference that describes structure. This is the dichotomy most likely to be misunderstood. It describes whether a person brings a judging or a perceiving preference to their outer, external (extroverted) world and therefore is the one most obviously on display for the outer world to see.

In this framework, Judging does not mean judgmental, nor does Perceiving mean perceptive (as in insightful about people and events). In preference-speak, Judging means this type prefers to have decisions (aka judgments) behind them (settled). They feel more comfortable once the decision, whatever it is, is made. In preference-speak, Perceiving means "preferring to take in information." Perceivers prefer to postpone decisions in order to stay open to new information as long as possible.

Judging types are in danger of missing new information because they're too focused on closure, on achieving the goal. These types plan ahead so they don't have to rush before deadlines. They are systematic, methodical, and scheduled.

Perceiving types are ever on the lookout for new information, often without even realizing they're doing it because it's second nature. To others, they appear flexible and spontaneous, and they don't like to have a lot of plans on the calendar.

Perceivers are in danger of staying open to new information for so long that they miss the opportunity to make a decision at all.

This preference is pretty evenly distributed in the general population, with a possible slight preference for Judging.[5]

The Sixteen MBTI Types in a Nutshell

Now that we've outlined the four dichotomies, we can start to see how those with various types are different not only in their behaviors but also in their values and points of view.

ISTJ	ISFJ	INFJ	INTJ
ISTP	ISFP	INFP	INTP
ESTP	ESFP	ENFP	ENTP
ESTJ	ESFJ	ENFJ	ENTJ

Let's take a quick look at the sixteen MBTI types. I've written one-paragraph summaries here, but you can find a ton of good information in books and online to dive deeper into the types.[6]

NT types (Keirsey's Rationals)

INTJ: The INTJ is a strategic thinker whose mind not only understands concepts but also is able to apply those concepts in useful ways. I can see author and apologist C. S.

Lewis as an INTJ. Both highly creative and intensely logical, Lewis was able to build deeply symbolic fantasy worlds from scratch, imbue ancient myths with even more significance in his adult fiction, and stake his claim as *the* Christian apologist of the mid-twentieth century with his clear, systematic defense of his faith.

INTP: The INTP is a curiosity-driven analyst who lives in the world of possibility, inventing theories for everything. I enjoy imagining that Jane Austen was an INTP, because she was a keen observer of life who relished exposing inconsistencies in her characters' behaviors. From her letters, historians gather this isn't a skill she confined to the page.

ENTP: The ENTP is a visionary who is constantly seeing possibilities in the world around them. The most interesting ENTP I've come across in a book lately is Mark Watney, the astronaut accidentally abandoned on Mars in Andy Weir's novel *The Martian*. ENTPs are great at improvising on the spot, finding creative solutions to problems new and old, and spotting logical fallacies in plans and systems—all qualities that kept Watney alive during his extended stay on the Red Planet.

ENTJ: The ENTJ is a natural-born leader whose forceful, decisive nature makes it easy for them to take charge. I see ENTJ qualities in Edward Rochester, the hero of Charlotte Brontë's novel *Jane Eyre* (if we can call someone who locks his wife in the attic a "hero"). He's confident and commanding; he makes his plan and deliberately carries it out; he uses his experiences to develop his own set of laws to live by.

NF Types (Keirsey's Idealists)

INFJ: The INFJ is a tireless idealist who is guided by a strong inner sense of right and wrong. Picture Atticus Finch in *To Kill a Mockingbird*. Atticus is that rare combination (truly, because INFJs make up less than 1 percent of the population) of idealism and action. Though soft-spoken, he will fight to the death for what he believes in and strives to see the world made right on both a large and a small scale.

INFP: The INFP is a creative dreamer whose inner imagination guides their values, beliefs, and actions. Anne Shirley from *Anne of Green Gables* is a textbook INFP—an idealistic kindred spirit who lives more in her dream world than in the real world. She's a hopeless romantic who's committed to her ideals and guided by pure intentions, even if reality isn't always sunshine and rainbows.

ENFP: The ENFP is a warm, inspiring enthusiast whose passion for projects and ideas is contagious. Picture Bridget Jones of *Bridget Jones's Diary*. Bridget is a free spirit. She's fond of witty banter and enthusiastic about everything. She may seem flighty, but she's always searching for the deeper meaning behind everything.

ENFJ: The ENFJ is a charismatic persuader whose excellent people skills can be used to influence, inspire, and motivate. Emma Woodhouse of Jane Austen's *Emma* just might be my favorite ENFJ. Handsome, clever, and rich (though only one of the three is an ENFJ trait), Emma relishes the spotlight, tells a great story, loves to exert her influence to "improve" others, and enjoys making connections between ideas and—more significantly—people.

SJ Types (Keirsey's Guardians)

ISTJ: The ISTJ is a quiet pillar of society with a deep regard for duty, tradition, and stability. It's clear to me that Marilla Cuthbert in *Anne of Green Gables* is absolutely an ISTJ. I can also see Colonel Brandon of Jane Austen's *Sense and Sensibility* as this type. He is dependable, objective, and realistic and has great respect for the past—all qualities that lead Willoughby to call him a bore but help him win over Marianne in the end.

ISFJ: The ISFJ is a kind-hearted nurturer who unites strong powers of observation with a deep-seated desire to do good. Mother Teresa seems like a good fit for this type, with her practical solutions and heavy reliance on what has worked in the past. This quote makes her sound like an ISFJ: "Don't look for big things; just do small things with great love."[7]

ESTJ: The ESTJ is an excellent administrator whose clear standards and values make this type a decisive, confident leader. Minerva McGonagall in J. K. Rowling's *Harry Potter* novels screams ESTJ to me. Her outer persona is confident, structured, and firm. She's quick with the wry comeback. In the words of David B. Goldstein and Otto Kroeger, "ESTJs are ingenious in solving real-world problems in practical, elegant, no-nonsense ways."[8] *That's* McGonagall all over.

ESFJ: The ESFJ is a people person who is genuinely interested in bringing out the best in others. Picture Margaret Hale in Elizabeth Gaskell's novel *North and South*. Margaret is resistant to change and sentimental about the loss of her old, idyllic life. She has zero qualms about calling out injustice when she sees it, and she doesn't hesitate to share her righteous opinions with others.

SP Types (Keirsey's Artisans)

ISTP: The ISTP is a hands-on master craftsman who is compelled to figure out how things work and is comfortable with tools of any kind. It's no coincidence that many action-hero types on the big screen, such as James Bond, present as ISTPs. Bond stays detached, keeps his cool, thinks on his feet, doesn't care about the rules, and is always ready to spring into action.

ISFP: The ISFP is an artist who is firmly grounded in reality and always up for experiencing something new. I see cartoonist Charles Schulz and his best-known character, Charlie Brown, as ISFPs. ISFPs, who rely on feeling and sensing, are very perceptive about the people around them; Schulz channeled his insights about human nature into his cartoons. Schulz himself was quiet, kind, and humble—all ISFP traits.

ESTP: The ESTP is an outgoing risk-taker who lives in the here and now and prefers to learn by doing. If anyone enjoys living on the edge, it's the ESTP. Imagine Scarlett O'Hara, the belle of the ball in *Gone with the Wind*, who delights in being the center of attention. Scarlett can turn on the charm or be intensely practical (or both at once, if you consider her marriages or the famous green dress she made out of Tara's curtains to seduce Rhett Butler).

ESFP: The ESFP is an entertainer at heart whose enthusiasm and energy often make them the center of attention. I can see Truman Capote, author of *Breakfast at Tiffany's* and *In Cold Blood*, as an ESFP, because of the way he approached both his work and his personal life. Capote felt he couldn't write *In Cold Blood*, which was based on a real event that happened in Kansas, until he visited the town and got to know the people involved.[9] In his social life, he basked in the attention of the elite New York society women he called his "swans."

You Are One, and Only One, Type

You may see yourself as fitting into one of three or four different types. But according to the MBTI, you are one type, not a hybrid. So banish that talk of being an INFP/J. Your MBTI type isn't just four mix-and-match letters; it describes a whole pattern of behavior and mindset. While no MBTI type description will perfectly capture everything about you, one will be closer than all the others.

Changing just one letter doesn't feel like a big deal, but that one letter can make a huge difference. Two types just one letter apart might not share *any* cognitive functions! (I've tried hard not to use that phrase until now. If what I just said makes zero sense to you, hang tight—we're getting there.)

Putting This Information to Work in Your Own Life

The MBTI is focused on personal growth. At its core, it assumes that self-understanding leads to growth. The MBTI makes you feel special, and at the same time it makes you feel as though you're not alone.

The MBTI assessment is a staple of colleges, corporate America, and career counselors, precisely as Briggs and Myers envisioned in the World War II era.

Many individuals first encounter the MBTI in their school days, since colleges and universities around the world use the assessment. Not many twenty-year-olds know what they want to do with their lives, even though they're in school to prepare for exactly that. That's where the MBTI assessment comes in. Understanding your type can be a huge shortcut to important decisions such as choosing a field of study and finding the right career path. The instrument helps students deliberately assess who they are, what they want, what they need, and how they are apt to succeed *before* they have to decide whether to study law or medicine; if they'd be happier moving to Chicago or Los Angeles; or if they should accept the start-up job offer or the corporate gig. The very process of wrestling through the inventory's questions forces people into a useful posture of self-awareness and self-examination. It's helpful on a personal level too. So many young people may feel they're a mess, especially if they're one of the rarer types. When a person identifies and learns about their type, they discover it's okay to be themselves.

The MBTI is a favorite workplace tool for similar reasons. Career counselors use it because when a person understands their personality, they can better identify which fields they'd probably be effective and happy in. This is because a person's work is so intimately connected to their talents, needs, and gifts.

Eighty-nine of the Fortune 100 companies use the assessment.[10] It's not unusual for potential hires to take an MBTI assessment as part of the employee vetting process. Corporations use it with the goal of helping their employees be the best they can be and aiding groups in working more effectively together by drawing on each individual's unique contributions to the organization. A broad distribution of type strengthens an organization and prevents it from being lopsided. Without all the types working together, an organization will have points of weakness. Using the MBTI mediates weaknesses by bringing the right people—and their accompanying strengths—on board.

Marriage counselors often lean on the MBTI because it helps people better understand themselves and their spouses. It gives them a neutral lens through which to view the ways they interact—both the wonderful ways and the stormy ones. As marriage expert John Gottman says, most conflicts in marriage aren't solvable; the best we can do is learn to manage them and live with them.[11] The MBTI has a similar assumption: a person's personality can't be changed, but it can be cultivated, and a variety of skills can be learned to facilitate better communication. Because the MBTI promotes empathy and understanding between individuals, it is an excellent tool for helping married people manage those unavoidable conflicts.

It's a valuable tool, but it's also frequently misunderstood and misapplied. Let's change that.

How (and How Not) to Determine Your Type

A shocking amount of confusion exists about the best way to go about finding your type in regard to the MBTI.

Online assessments abound, and many people attempt to determine their type using one of the copious unofficial assessments available. People love these because they're fast, free, and easy. And while they *are* a good starting point, don't put too much faith in your results.

Why? Because it's amazingly easy to mistype yourself. I've spoken with many people who say they get a different answer every time they take an online test, leading them to believe their personality type changed. That's not what's going on.

The truth is, like me, they didn't type themselves correctly in the first place. The Myers & Briggs Foundation requires the official instrument to be administered by a trained professional to ensure that you get what it calls your best-fit type, and it strongly suggests a follow-up conversation with a knowledgeable MBTI expert.[12]

I took the official MBTI assessment just a couple years ago—long past the point when I knew better—and typed myself completely wrong. It was the official instrument, but the person administering the assessment was a lay enthusiast, not a trained MBTI administrator, and I'm positive that made a difference. I tested as an INTJ, when I'm really an INFP. You might remember I made this same mistake when I took the official assessment back in college. Back then I made the mistake of answering the questions based on what I wanted to be like, not what I really was like. When I screwed up the test recently, it was because I answered the questions according to my learned behaviors, not according to my inborn preferences. These learned behaviors do not affect my MBTI type.

The error rate of people who are mistyped is caused by several factors. First, as a self-reporting instrument, it's only as accurate as a person's answers. Second, the official instrument's questions are quite straightforward, almost misleadingly so. It can be hard to understand exactly what the assessment is asking. Takers often don't understand that they need to answer with their gut-level reactions to generate an accurate result. You want the response that best captures who you are at your core—without molding, shaping, or training. For the test to be accurate, you need to pinpoint your *innate* behavior, not your *learned* behavior. By the time you have a few decades behind you, untangling the two can be difficult!

Vocabulary can also play a role in incorrect results. The assessment uses familiar words (*extravert, perceptive, sensing*) in unfamiliar ways, and this understandable vocabulary confusion can generate inaccurate results.

Environmental factors can also skew your results. Your mood and fatigue level at the time you take the assessment will affect its outcome.

A paid version of the official assessment is, of course, available on the internet,[13] but if you want to take the official instrument, the easiest way may be to get in touch with your closest career counseling center. You'll be able to significantly close the 20 percent error gap by talking over the instrument with a trained MBTI administrator, both before you take the test and after you get your results. (Hopefully reading this book will also improve your odds of getting an accurate result!) You should have the foundation you need to understand your type after reading this book and talking things over with someone who knows you well.

If you prefer to figure out your results on your own, tread carefully. Some MBTI experts specifically advise against reading the various type descriptions available online and elsewhere to help you determine your type. They believe those descriptions are misleading and confusing, more like horoscopes than diagnostic tools. I've found the descriptions useful myself; they've helped me build a framework for understanding the different types of personalities, making it easier for me to perceive the wide variety of healthy human behavior at work in me and the people around me.

When trying to identify your type, remember that no one MBTI type description will perfectly capture everything about you. The question to ask yourself is, Which type fits me better than any of the others?

If you want to go the free route, I prefer the short, simple test at www.16personalities.com,[14] but remember—as we discussed earlier—your results are only a starting point.

A few guidelines for taking the self-test:

1. Answer each question *quickly*. Give it five to seven seconds. If you don't know the answer, move on and come back to it later.

2. Give your gut-level answer. No overthinking.

3. Be honest with yourself. Give the true answer, not the answer you *wish* were true.

4. If you're not sure how to answer, ask yourself what you were like as a child. Select the answer that best applies to your grade-school self.

5. Do the best you can for now, because we're diving into more information on getting your type right in the next chapter.

Get Comfortable with Your Type Description

Once you have your type description in hand, it's time to read all about it. I've listed my favorite books in the Recommended Resources section. There's a huge amount of information online, but not all of it is good, so proceed with caution. My favorite MBTI descriptions on the internet can be found at personalitypage.com.[15]

You won't see yourself in every part of every description—I sure didn't. You may not even *like* parts of the descriptions. (I'm an INFP, and I hate the thought of anyone calling me a "healer," yet that's how my type is often described.) But don't skip this step, because it's a quick and easy way to see what your MBTI type could look like in action. After you read about common patterns of behavior for each type, you'll be able to more easily identify similar behaviors in your own life or in the lives of the people around you.

How (and How Not) to Use Your Type

Our types should never dictate who we are or what we do—not to ourselves or to anyone else. Maybe you've heard people say things such as, "I'm an ENFP, so I couldn't possibly _____." That is not the point of diving into the MBTI framework. Instead, we can use our MBTI types to gain clarity about aspects of our personalities that we have felt lingering beneath the surface but have never been able to articulate. Once we bring these things into the light, before our conscious minds, we can actually do something about them.

Some of these action points are practical. For instance, after my methodical friend helped me realize I wasn't a planner at all, I was able to face the fact that I wasn't great at managing my calendar and actually do something about it. I had been struggling in this area for years, but because I thought of myself as someone who was good at this, I was blind to my struggles. When the blinders came off, I was free to get the help I needed, which mainly meant asking friends who *are* natural planners to help me put systems in place.

Some of the actions I've taken are more personal. As I've learned about what it means to be an INFP, I've been able to recognize myself in descriptions of common but unhealthy behaviors. For example, INFPs are at risk of idealizing their important relationships and then getting really disappointed when the other people in these relationships inevitably disappoint them—not necessarily because they did something terrible but because they're human. Looking back over my life, I can see this pattern at work in ways that are much too embarrassing to put in the pages of this book.

Try this for another example. As an Idealist type, I can be quick to get caught up in the moment and say melodramatic things that I've learned the hard way I'll feel really stupid about later. I've discovered that even though this is my natural tendency, I don't have to go with it. I can bite my tongue and avoid feeling like a schmuck later when my easily enflamed emotions have died down.

The Good and the Bad about Your Type

I've hinted at the fact that each type has its strengths and weaknesses. Different types have different needs and differing expectations from life and people and bring different things to the table.

Let's say you are an ISFJ. The odds of this are pretty good; it's one of the most common types. You probably already know you're people-oriented and that you hold tightly to your core values. You're probably friendly, upbeat, and tradition-minded. You're responsible, practical, and family-oriented.

That's all good news, and a lot of MBTI talk stops right there, with the good stuff. But let's harness that information about your ISFJ type to take a look at your weaknesses—your blind spots. Blind spots are the problem points in our lives we never worry about because we don't even know they exist. When you learn about your type—the good and the bad—this knowledge can serve as your guardrail. It's much easier to keep from falling off the edge of the road if your eyes are wide open and the path is lit.

Potential blind spots for the ISFJ include: you're likely to be uncomfortable with change, whether that's a change of career or a change of apartment or a change of relationship, like a break-up. You care about the way things look, which can be a strength—until you cross the line into becoming overly status-conscious. You care a lot about what others think, and compared to other types, you may need more positive affirmation to feel good about yourself. If you're in an unhealthy place, you may not take good care of yourself, sacrificing your needs for those of others. You may catch yourself guilting others into doing what you want.

This is where the MBTI can help. If you're convinced you're not the kind of person who would ever manipulate someone into doing what you want, you won't even notice when you do it. But if, as you learn about your type, you shine a light on that blind spot, you'll be able to catch yourself in the act and *stop doing it* (well, at least some of the time).

As I've learned more about my type over the years, I've gotten comfortable with my strengths . . . and the weaknesses that go hand in hand with them. Just as you can't simultaneously be short *and* tall, whatever strengths each type has are offset by corresponding weaknesses.

As an INFP, I do ideas really well. I'm terrific at coming up with new concepts and possibilities. The flip side of this is that I'm not so great at the follow-through. But that doesn't mean INFPs never finish their projects. In their wonderful book *Creative You*, David B. Goldstein and Otto Kroeger explore the different styles of creativity among the sixteen MBTI types. The way they articulate the INFP's creative process has helped me. For my type, they write, "The possibilities are usually more exciting than the actual doing, and INFPs leave projects unstarted and unfinished. So you must step back and take a moment to consider how your ideas can be put into practice while focusing on deadlines and sharing; this amplifies your strengths."[16]

Ideally, interacting with the MBTI also will help you better understand how to interact with types who are different from your own. Once you learn how other types see the world, you'll find it easier to accept them for who they are and know how to respond when you interact. By learning more about typing, and the sixteen personality types, you can see how traits you once perceived as weaknesses may actually be strengths, and vice versa. There are two sides to every coin—each type has strengths and weaknesses, which result in wildly different careers, leadership styles, and more.

Working through Communication Breakdowns

When we bring different personality types together, communication breakdowns are inevitable. Communication is the main challenge we face when we interact closely with people of different types because each of us interprets, understands, and acts in different ways.

Thinking types may feel they're being considerate by getting straight to the point in a conversation, unaware that their feeling friends perceive them as uncomfortably blunt. Intuitive types may think they're contributing by sharing their grand plans in a team meeting, unaware that the thought of making so many changes at once completely stresses out their sensing colleagues. Extroverted types may feel disappointed when their spouses don't immediately respond with enthusiasm to their ideas, ignorant that they just need time to think the ideas over.

Because we have so much invested in our relationships, it can be enormously unsettling when they seem to go "wrong." Understanding the MBTI helps us see that misunderstandings are inevitable. When we don't see eye to eye with someone else, it doesn't mean things are going wrong—it means they're normal.

Conflicts that arise due to personality differences can be troublesome but fairly innocuous, as long as we're able to diagnose what's happening. Not all relational conflicts are personality conflicts, of course, but many are. And those can often be effectively managed when we enlist the aid of a good personality framework to see the world through someone else's eyes for a bit.

More than Meets the Eye

Many people find the MBTI to be an extraordinarily useful tool for understanding themselves, their work, their habits, and their relationships.

But for this type talk to be helpful, you need to get your type *right*—which, as we've covered, is difficult to do. This is the bad news for all you armchair MBTI geeks, because to really "get" framework, you have to understand what the cognitive functions are and how they operate. If you're confused about your MBTI type, this is probably why. In the next chapter, we'll dive into the lesser-known but extremely important cognitive functions, the heartbeat of the framework.

7

The Deck Is Stacked

the mbti cognitive functions

My friend Kim and I sat at my kitchen counter with an open laptop, two iced coffees, and a yellow legal pad.

Kim threw down the gauntlet. "I'm not getting up until you tell me my Myers-Briggs type once and for all." She'd taken every free test on the web and kept waffling between the types. "I just can't decide if I'm the entertainer or the entrepreneur," she said.

"What types are those?" I asked.

"One is Madonna and one is Marilyn Monroe."

"I mean, what are the letter combinations?"

Kim had no idea, so we fired up the website she'd been relying on. It turned out she was wavering between ESTP and ESFP.

"All the descriptions start to sound the same after a while. Are you sure I'm not both?" she asked. "How do I decide?"

I reached for my pen. I strongly suspected that Kim was struggling because she hadn't identified her cognitive functions. When you skip over the cognitive functions—and most people do—the MBTI info won't be as helpful as it could be. It might even be grossly misleading. That's because the only way to truly determine your MBTI type is to identify your functions and the order you use them in.

What You Need to Know about Cognitive Functions

I know the term "cognitive functions" sounds fancy, but it's just a short way of describing all the different ways our minds are capable of working—the ways our brains are wired. The functions identify the specific ways we process information and make decisions, depending on our individual personality types. Learning about cognitive functions is like learning a new language. It might sound like gibberish at first, but before long you won't have to give the shorthand notations a second thought. If you push through, you'll get the hang of it. Your understanding of the MBTI and how it works will grow exponentially, making it a much more effective and fascinating tool. Understanding the cognitive functions is not super simple, but it's worth it.

The Eight Cognitive Functions

Your type is not just a combination of letters; it's a pattern of mental behavior. To get the most accurate MBTI type for yourself, you need to identify the cognitive functions you rely on and the specific order you use them in. It's a surprise to many when they find out that this is in fact the whole point of the assessment. The end game isn't simply to label your preferences but to discover the mental processes that underpin your personality.

There are eight cognitive processes, or cognitive functions:

Perceptive Functions:

Extraverted Sensing (Se)	Extraverted Intuiting (Ne)
Introverted Sensing (Si)	Introverted Intuiting (Ni)

Judging Functions:

Extraverted Thinking (Te)	Extraverted Feeling (Fe)
Introverted Thinking (Ti)	Introverted Feeling (Fi)

As the above chart demonstrates, four functions are introverted, four are extraverted. The vocabulary here is important. Introverted simply means directed inwardly, toward the inner world. Extraverted means directed outwardly, toward the external world. These terms refer not to sociability but to each function's orientation toward the world.

In addition, four of the eight functions are perceptive; they help us take in, process, and make sense of new information. Their purpose is to explore possibilities. Four functions are judging (or decision-based) functions. They help us evaluate that information and make decisions based on it. These functions help us draw conclusions and make plans.

Everyone, regardless of type, has two perceptive functions and two judging functions. Everyone, regardless of type, has two extraverted functions and two introverted functions—the mental processes used on a daily basis. And everyone, regardless of type, has one intuitive function, one sensing function, one thinking function, and one feeling function.

The Order of Our Function Stack Matters

These functions don't just pop up randomly out of the function lotto machine. They work together in important ways. There's a hierarchy to function use. Every MBTI personality type's functions follow a certain order of operations, top to bottom, most used to least used, strongest to weakest:

Dominant (1st)
Auxiliary (2nd)
Tertiary (3rd)
Inferior (4th)

Because we take our dominant function for granted, two things happen: (1) we assume everyone interacts with the world the same way we do, and (2) we have a hard time perceiving our dominant function at work because we use it so effortlessly.

If you're an extrovert (meaning your MBTI type begins with E), then your dominant function is always extraverted. If you're an introvert (your MBTI type begins with I), then your dominant function is always introverted. Your auxiliary function is always the opposite orientation of your dominant function, meaning you—along with everyone else—have one extraverted function and one introverted function in your top two.

Now, let's talk about that auxiliary function. If your dominant function is your pilot, you can think of your auxiliary function as the copilot; it works with your dominant function as you move through life. As second best, this function is still awfully strong. In fact, it's more readily apparent to you than your first function because your auxiliary function requires conscious thought, unlike the dominant function, which you use intuitively.

And for introverts—because their auxiliary function is always extraverted—it's the function most obviously on display to the world. This is a major reason why introverts often feel misunderstood: the biggest piece of their personality identity is literally hidden. Other people truly can't see the dominant process guiding everything they do. The truth is that we're all a little bit of everything. We're all Sensers, Feelers, Intuitives, etc. The real questions are, Which kind (introverted or extraverted) are you and in what order? And how do those functions work together?

The Eight Cognitive Functions Explained

Let's explore what each function means so you can figure out which ones make up your deck. What do these processes look like at work?

Pay special attention to which functions you resonate with and notice the variety of mental processes. A key insight will be how many people's minds work differently from yours.

As I think about how these functions work, it helps me to imagine them as eight software programs, humming along—with their own individual prerogatives and priorities—in my brain.

To avoid being overwhelmed, I recommend sticking to the functions you think might be in *your* cognitive stack on your first read-through. You can come back and read about your friends' and loved ones' functions after you've absorbed the information a little.

Perceptive Functions (Ne, Ni, Se, Si)

Intuition is a perceptive function, which means it's about learning/gathering information.

143

Extraverted Intuition (Ne): Extraverted Intuition is an expansive function that imagines possibilities, synthesizes ideas, and draws connections between seemingly unrelated things. It enjoys brainstorming, speculating, and connecting ideas to one another. Extraverted Intuition is future-oriented, focusing on what could happen next instead of what's happening now or what happened in the past. This function excels at exploring every possible angle or side of an issue, a skill that makes it difficult for people who rely heavily on Extraverted Intuition to find closure in the decision-making process.

People who lead with Extraverted Intuition—that is, who use Extraverted Intuition as their dominant function—are great at seeing possibilities and patterns of meaning. They are light-hearted, spontaneous, and extremely open-minded—sometimes to a fault. They are great starters, but they see so many ideas that it's difficult for them to pick one and stick with it. They may seem distractible or "bouncy," because one idea always leads them to another.

Introverted Intuition (Ni): Introverted Intuition builds a framework to explain how the world works, drawing on detailed, abstract analysis of current and past events. This function is great at simplifying ideas to their core, working convergently to narrow all available options to a single comprehensive solution. Introverted Intuition is future-oriented: this function is excellent at visualizing likely or best outcomes for future events, as opposed to what's currently happening. This cognitive process excels at seeing patterns of behavior and cause and effect and using those patterns to anticipate what's coming next.

People who lead with Introverted Intuition are excellent problem solvers who love to generate theories. They are highly

144

perceptive, insightful, and great at spotting logical fallacies and inconsistencies. They trust their intuition and their hunches.

Sensing is a perceptive function, which means it's about learning/gathering information.

Extraverted Sensing (Se): Extraverted Sensing is focused on what's happening right here, right now. More so than any other function, Extraverted Sensing is in the moment. It's fantastic at taking in information through the five senses, registering everything that's happening. Extraverted Sensing is attuned to the external world, taking in raw data in the form of information gathered through the five senses.

People who lead with Extraverted Sensing are sensation-seekers who love the new and novel. They have a hands-on approach to life, live in the present, and think fast on their feet. They are naturally impulsive and confident and have an appreciation for aesthetics. They're good at absorbing sensual experiences and gathering facts, but they're not prone to overanalyzing situations.

Introverted Sensing (Si): Introverted Sensing is a detail-oriented function that is great at storing data and information, neatly filing them away, as in a filing system. It's oriented toward the past, focusing more on what has been than on what will be. Introverted Sensing takes an inward, reflective focus as it relies on this stored information from the past to understand the present.

Those who lead with Introverted Sensing respect tradition, uphold the status quo, and do things by the book. They are organized and structured. They prefer routines and predictability and have a tendency toward nostalgia. More than any other type, they believe the past repeats itself.

Judging/Decision-Making Functions (Fe, Fi, Te, Ti)

Feeling is a judging function, which means it's about decision-making. This isn't just about emotions; it's prioritizing how a decision will affect people before considering the cold, hard facts. Imagine a judge delivering a verdict.

Extraverted Feeling (Fe): Extraverted Feeling prioritizes maintaining harmony in the external environment. It is focused on helping everyone get along and strives to do what is best for the group as a whole. More so than any other function, Extraverted Feeling requires social interaction to be satisfied. Extraverted Feeling is quick to read and empathize with the emotions of others.

People who lead with Extraverted Feeling wear their hearts on their sleeves. They are quick to display their feelings and opinions and equally quick to turn to others for emotional support. They can't fully relax unless those around them are happy and healthy. They are highly reactive to other people's feelings and prone to reflecting others' emotions back to them. They are expressive, accommodating, and sensitive to criticism.

Introverted Feeling (Fi): Introverted Feeling is focused inwardly on the abstract world of thoughts, feelings, and values. This function aims to discover the deeper meaning behind everything by deeply reflecting on and analyzing emotions as fully as possible. Introverted Feeling demands authenticity, seeking consistency between what it believes and what it does. It's also extremely empathetic to the feelings of others.

People who lead with Introverted Feeling are in touch with their emotions. They are compassionate and analytical and have a strong sense of right and wrong. They are often highly creative or artistic and prone to feeling misunderstood. They

146

have a rich inner world and feel deeply, but because this function is introverted, they're not always comfortable expressing how they feel and don't wear their hearts on their sleeves.

Thinking is a judging function, which means it's about decision-making.

Extraverted Thinking (Te): Extraverted Thinking is a results-based, action-oriented function that focuses on what *is*. It excels at executing ideas in external reality and imposing order on the external environment in an efficient and logical way. This function values productivity and usefulness and is great at foreseeing consequences and getting from point A to point B.

People who lead with Extraverted Thinking are pragmatic, analytical, decisive, and skilled at building logical arguments. They tend to be black-and-white thinkers; unlike others, the boundaries aren't blurry for them. They are quick to take charge and don't mind confrontation. They like to get their ideas out and hear feedback. While they may appear to be bossy and opinionated, they believe they're helping everyone by pointing out the most efficient plan.

Introverted Thinking (Ti): Introverted Thinking is focused inwardly on the abstract world of reason. It seeks to understand how things work and builds a framework for understanding the world by discovering the logical principles that support it. This function is great at organizing ideas and naturally notices inconsistencies.

People who lead with Introverted Thinking are self-disciplined, logical, and objective. They are great at thinking deeply about every angle of an idea, examining every detail, and figuring out how all the pieces fit together. They are skilled at spotting ways to make a system more efficient. They are nonconfrontational and may appear detached, and as though they live in their own heads.

Our Mental Processes Grow with Us

As we mature, our mental processes mature as well. When we're young, we have little control over or access to our weaker functions. We mostly inadvertently turn to our tertiary and auxiliary functions in times of stress. But that changes with time. If you feel as though you're becoming more well-rounded over time, as most people do, it's because your weaker functions are predictably strengthening. Our cognitive processes develop chronologically according to our personal hierarchies.

For most of us, the tertiary function finally becomes readily apparent in our twenties, and the inferior function doesn't typically develop until we're nearing middle age. Although, interestingly, stress or challenging emotional seasons can prompt our weaker functions to develop sooner.

Many of us notice that our personalities seem to shift as we move into our twenties and thirties and chalk it up to our MBTI type changing because we're maturing or we got married or we had kids or we took a new job. That's not what happens. We don't change our MBTI type, but we develop and strengthen those processes that characterize our type that are already present. We become deeper, more complete versions of ourselves.

The inferior function is our weakest link, the one we're least proficient with. It's also the subject of some very interesting psychological theories. Jung believed the inferior function was the "bridge" between the conscious personality and the world of the unconscious and that when our inferior function "erupted" (as in times of stress), it provided helpful and interesting insights into the personality. Naomi Quenk wrote a book about how we act when we're in the grip of our inferior function called, tellingly, *Was That Really Me?*, in which she examines how and why we're all inclined to go off the rails in predictable ways during stressful times.

Accessing the inferior function is not easy (except in times of provocation or stress, when it may erupt, prompting behavior that baffles us because it's so unlike our usual selves). And integrating our inferior function into our whole selves is even more difficult. However, for those of us who are able to do so, learning how to access that inferior function can help us become the best—and most complete—versions of ourselves.

Putting This Information to Work in Your Own Life

Now that we have more information about the cognitive functions, let's explore what the MBTI types *really* mean. Here's what the function stack looks like for each of the sixteen MBTI personality types:

Cognitive Function Hierarchy

ISTJ	ISFJ	INFJ	INTJ
Si	Si	Ni	Ni
Te	Fe	Fe	Te
Fi	Ti	Ti	Fi
Ne	Ne	Se	Se
ISTP	ISFP	INFP	INTP
Ti	Fi	Fi	Ti
Se	Se	Ne	Ne
Ni	Ni	Si	Si
Fe	Te	Te	Fe

ESTP	ESFP	ENFP	ENTP
Se	Se	Ne	Ne
Ti	Fi	Fi	Ti
Fe	Te	Te	Fe
Ni	Ni	Si	Si
ESTJ	**ESFJ**	**ENFJ**	**ENTJ**
Te	Fe	Fe	Te
Si	Si	Ni	Ni
Ne	Ne	Se	Se
Fi	Ti	Ti	Fi

If you have a decent idea of what your MBTI type is, find yourself on this chart and jot down your cognitive function stack. Then go back and read through the descriptions of what each of these mental processes involves and imagine how they might work together to make you *you*. If these descriptions resonate, congratulations! You've typed yourself correctly. If they feel off, you've probably gotten your type wrong. But don't despair! When you develop a working knowledge of cognitive functions, the likelihood that you'll get your MBTI right skyrockets.

Determining Your Type with the Cognitive Functions

Let's go back to my friend Kim, who couldn't decide if she was an ESTP or an ESFP. While we sat at my kitchen counter, we made a chart showing the cognitive function stack for each type.

ESTP vs. ESFP

Se	Se
Ti	Fi
Fe	Te
Ni	Ni

"It's no wonder you're confused," I said, drawing circles around the two Se and Ni notations. "These two types are similar. They have the same dominant function and the same inferior function. Both types lead with Extraverted Sensing, which means you focus on the here and now and are fantastic at taking in information through your five senses. People with Extraverted Sensing love the new and novel. They are hands-on and have a strong aesthetic sense. Does that sound like you?"

Kim nodded. She's an engineer by training, and she runs a sewing business. She loves to take apart store-bought handbags and figure out how to make them herself at home. This made perfect sense.

I agreed. That sounded exactly like her.

"But the next-best function—which you still use all the time—is different for the two types. So is the third function. When we nail these, we'll have your type.

"If you're an ESTP, your auxiliary is Introverted Thinking. This cognitive function wants to know how things work. It's great at understanding systems and organizing ideas. This function is able to see how all the pieces fit together."

Kim laughed. "I think I use that function every day."

"If you're an ESFP, your auxiliary function is Introverted Feeling. That function seeks to discover the deeper meaning behind everything. It's a reflective process that analyzes emotions and wants to experience authenticity between what you believe and what you do."

"Um, that's not really me," Kim said.

I didn't think so, either.

We took a look at Kim's third function to be sure, and before we stood up, Kim had confidently declared herself an ESTP (Se-Ti-Fe-Ni). That's the entrepreneur, in case you were wondering, but it's not the label that matters. It's the functions—which ones do we utilize and in what order?

Let's break it down.

Here's what Kim's cognitive function stack looks like in action. When Extroverted Sensing (Se) is in charge, it wants to fully engage with all the sensory aspects of any experience—what can be tasted, seen, smelled, heard, or touched. Introverted Thinking (Ti) is copilot, evaluating the logical systems in the environment and identifying ways they can be put into action. Extraverted Feeling (Fe) is next in line, which is the ability to read other people's motivations and emotions. Introverted Intuition (Ni) completes the stack. In the inferior position, it shows up as a profound dislike for overanalysis.

The Functions at Work in You

Now that I understand the cognitive functions and have identified my function stack, I can spot the functions at work in myself. As an INFP, I have a stack that looks like this:

Dominant:	Introverted Feeling
Auxiliary:	Extraverted Intuition
Tertiary:	Introverted Sensing
Inferior:	Extraverted Thinking

When it came to my dominant Introverted Feeling, I used to be the fish who didn't know what water was—it was such a part of my environment that I had never thought about it. Now I can *see* when my Introverted Feeling is firing. As evidence, I present my first-draft conclusion to this chapter. This paragraph was composed by Introverted Feeling.

Let's stop to appreciate the variety of mental processes available to all of us and pause to remember that on our best days we probably bring only two to the table. What a wonderful, diverse world it is—full of people who share our point of view and even more people who see the world in *an entirely different way*. The world is a better place for these differences, and it's always important to remember this.

Notice how very Introverted Feeling this is? The argument focuses on thoughts, feelings, and values. It points the reader toward the deeper meaning behind everything, urging consistency between what one believes (*Isn't the world a great place with all these different types?*) and what one does (*Appreciate it, darn it!*).

That's a bit mushy for my taste—and I'm the one who wrote it! Thank goodness I have other functions in my stack. Introverted Feeling may be my dominant function, but Extroverted Intuition is my favorite. It's the one that loves to travel and explore and try new things out in the world—books or food or cities or hiking trails. It lets me see a situation from every possible angle. It's why I love discussing big-picture ideas.

In my thirties, I'm finally learning to recognize the functions at the bottom of my stack. I can see tertiary Introverted Sensing kick in when I get hopelessly sentimental, when I'm accurately remembering tiny details, and when I somehow manage to be detail-oriented (for once) when I'm working on a project that's important to me. And Extroverted Thinking, my inferior function, is at work when I'm forming persuasive arguments and following through on plans and projects.

Don't Give Up!

The cognitive functions can sound intimidating at first. But if you want to embrace the full benefits of the Myers-Briggs framework, don't give up. Your efforts will pay off. First of all, understanding the cognitive functions allows you to be confident of your MBTI type. But more than that, it gives you one more tool in your toolbox to help you understand why people behave the way they do and what to do about it, whether that person is you or someone else.

My J friends have introduced me to a favorite tool of organizing junkies: the label maker. One friend even helped me label the files in my office to make things easier to find. Labeling everything is a tiny bit of a pain, but it's worth it in the end. Just as I've learned to label my file folders and boxes, I've learned to label certain types of my behavior. Sorting your behaviors into the right boxes can help you understand what you're great at and why, what you need to thrive and how you can get more of it, and what sorts of tasks make you crazy and what to do about it.

The point isn't to trap you in those boxes; it's to organize your behavior in a way that makes sense and helps you understand how the pieces work together, how to find them when you need them, and how to put them to work in pursuit of your best self.

8

Play to Your Strengths

the clifton strengthsfinder

"I've always enjoyed reading, but it was the StrengthsFinder that made me *love* reading."

I looked at my friend in surprise. I knew the StrengthsFinder, but I'd never heard anyone give it credit for something like this before. "I don't understand how that's possible," I said. "What happened?"

"Well, when I took the StrengthsFinder assessment, I found out my biggest talent is Input. I use that for my job every day, but I'd never thought to apply it to the books I read on my own time."

"So how did you make the connection?"

"Two things. First, when I got the results, they explained that my brain is basically a very thirsty sponge that wants to soak up all kinds of interesting information about *everything*. And that's true—I love learning new things."

"What else?" I asked.

"My results said reading is a big way to feed my Input talent. It suddenly made sense to me that even though reading my monthly book club pick can be a drag—it's usually some new, popular novel—I love learning new information from the books I read. I started picking my books with that in mind."

"And that changed the way you feel about reading?"

"It totally did. Now that I'm reading in the way that's right for me, it's one of my favorite things."

Initially, I was surprised the StrengthsFinder assessment had made such a big difference in my friend's reading life. But I shouldn't have been. She was using it in exactly the way it was intended. It helped her identify what she was already naturally good at and showed her how to bring more of it into her life. That is the assessment's mission in a nutshell.

What You Need to Know about the Clifton StrengthsFinder

Back in 1998, Tom Rath and a team of Gallup scientists, led by Donald O. Clifton, began working on a framework that would focus on human strengths. According to Rath, "We were tired of living in a world that revolved around fixing our weaknesses."[1] They wanted to start a conversation about how people could grow by building their talents instead of punishing their weaknesses. The assessment is built on the general model of positive psychology. That means the assessment doesn't care about what might be "wrong" with you; instead, it focuses on what's already working.

In 2001, the first version of the assessment was published in the bestselling book *Now, Discover Your Strengths*. That version is now known as StrengthsFinder 1.0; the version that's still in use today was published in 2007 in the book *StrengthsFinder 2.0*. The creators envisioned the tool being used in the workplace. They imagined employees and managers using it in multiperson team settings. Individuals' strengths are often featured in potential employees' résumés, published on organizational charts, and discussed in employee performance reviews. The assessment is also often used as a coaching tool in corporate settings. While it continues to be used for this purpose, StrengthsFinder is also used in communities, schools, and organizations, and new books have been published with a wider reach, such as *Strengths-Based Parenting* and *StrengthsExplorer for Kids Ages 10–14*, and *Strengths-Based Marriage*.

Because of its history and present applications, Strengths Finder is often talked about in terms of work, but if you don't have a day job, don't sweat it. Think of work as "the stuff you have to get done." (That highly technical definition is my own.) We *all* engage in work, whatever that looks like, and the StrengthsFinder assessment can help us see how our strengths fit into all that stuff.

We all have different talents and bring different things to the table. And we are all happiest when we get to capitalize on our strengths and be appreciated for them. Some of us put those strengths to work at the office because we're working on a team in a corporate setting, but if our lives don't look like that, we still want to feel like we're making a meaningful contribution! When we understand our strengths, we are better able to understand why we may be particularly suited to being a stay-at-home mom or making things happen in our church committee or handling logistics for the neighborhood council. When we understand our gifts, we can clearly see why it's so important to us to tick things off our to-do lists or make introductions between friends or dream up new ideas.

The StrengthsFinder's premise is that we are *not* well-rounded. Instead, it assumes we have a kaleidoscope of strengths and helps us not only identify what we are good at but also pinpoint exactly what kind of work we would be happiest doing. In stark contrast to much motivational literature, a bedrock StrengthsFinder assumption is that it's not possible to be anything we want to be— but it *is* possible to cultivate a lot more of what we already are.

Talents Come Naturally; Strengths Must Be Developed

The StrengthsFinder is built around thirty-four "talent themes." Talents come naturally; these are the ways we naturally think, feel, and act. Perhaps, without trying, we're naturally outgoing at social events or we're compassionate and empathetic when a friend cries on our shoulder or we're flexible when plans change at the last minute. These are talents.

The StrengthsFinder helps us identify, understand, and build on our naturally occurring talents to create areas of strength. (Technically, the assessment tool helps us identify *talents*, not strengths.) A strength is something we're flat-out *awesome* at. If "awesome" isn't technical enough for you, the StrengthsFinder defines a strength as "the ability to consistently provide near-perfect performance" in a given activity.[2] The ability to explain a complicated financial statement to a client is a strength. So is the ability to feed and clothe a large family on a tight budget or write a funny and thoughtful personal letter to a friend.

158

(Although some people would say that last one is an obsolete strength. Maybe I should say "email" instead of "letter"?)

Some of these talents may come so naturally to us that we don't realize not everyone has them. Others may feel so foreign that we don't realize *anyone* could have these capabilities.

An Overview of the Thirty-Four Themes or Strengths

The StrengthsFinder identifies possible themes that capture our motivations, interpersonal skills, and learning styles. Through a series of questions, the assessment identifies our top five themes—that is, areas of potential strength—from among all these possibilities.

The thirty-four themes are broken down into four loose categories: executing, influencing, relationship building, and strategic thinking. Here is an overview of how people demonstrate each of these themes.

Executing Themes

Achiever. Driven to work hard, enjoy being busy and productive, and want to have something to show for their efforts at the end of every single day.

Activator. Great at making things happen.

Adaptability. Flexible and present-oriented. They're able not only to respond to changing needs and circumstances but also to enjoy it.

Belief. Hold tight to their core values, which inform everything they do. They are consistent and dependable.

Discipline. Fight life's numerous distractions by insisting on routine, order, and predictability.

Focus. Need clear goals to stay on track with their work. With the right goals in place, they are single-minded and efficient.

Restorative. Love to fix things when they break, either literally or metaphorically. They are energized by the challenge of diagnosing problems and finding solutions.

Self-Assurance. Have faith not only in their abilities but also in the unique perspective they know they alone bring to the world. (Self-assurance goes beyond self-confidence.)

Significance. Yearn to be recognized by others. This yearning is a key motivation for their hard work.

Influencing Themes

Command. Have no qualms about taking charge. They are natural leaders who aren't afraid to make decisions or be confrontational when they deem it necessary.

Competition. Cannot help but measure success in comparison to others. They love to win, but they also love competition for its own sake.

Developer. Can recognize and cultivate the potential they see in others.

Maximizer. Want to make the most of what they've been given. They're not satisfied with making something good—they won't be happy unless they make something *great*.

Positivity. Naturally positive, upbeat, and energetic—and their enthusiasm is contagious.

Woo. This stands for "winning others over." They enjoy meeting new people and securing their approval, admiration, or friendship.

Relationship-Building Themes

Communication. Driven to present abstract ideas in a way that other people can understand and get excited about, whether they do this by making a presentation, talking to a coworker, or using the written word.

Empathy. Instinctively understand how others are feeling.

Harmony. Want everyone to get along. They seek to build consensus by looking for areas of agreement.

Includer. Naturally accepting and want everyone to feel like they're part of the group.

Individualization. Believe every individual possesses unique qualities and seek to understand these qualities so they can draw out the best in others.

Relator. Drawn to people they already know. They crave genuine relationships and particularly yearn to deepen their existing relationships.

Responsibility. Take ownership of everything they say, do, and commit to. When they take on a task, there's no question they will get it done.

Strategic-Thinking Themes

Analytical. Logical, rigorous, and objective. They are excellent at formulating and recognizing sound theories and ideas.

Arranger. Brilliant with managing all the variables of a given situation into the best possible plan. They are characterized by strong organizational skills *and* flexibility.

Connectedness. Believe that at some level we are all connected. This deep trust in the underlying unity of all people makes them compassionate and empathetic, as well as excellent bridge builders between those with opposing points of view.

Consistency. Believe it's important to treat everyone the same, regardless of how important or influential they may or may not be in the eyes of others.

Context. Feel as though they must understand the past to understand the present.

Deliberative. Reserved and cautious, they move slowly and carefully through life, constantly on guard against potential risks, knowing the potential for error is everywhere.

Futuristic. Future-oriented, meaning they're more inspired by what could be than what is. Future possibilities excite them, and they are able to get others excited about these possibilities too.

Ideation. Fascinated by ideas and especially enjoy drawing connections between seemingly disparate things.

Input. Curious types who love taking in new information about anything and everything, for no other reason than that the world is full of interesting information.

Intellection. Enjoy the mental hum of serious thinking.

Learner. Enjoy the learning process. They find satisfaction in the journey from ignorance to mastery.

Strategic. Adept at identifying the best way forward amidst a sea of possible paths.

Taking the Assessment

The StrengthsFinder assessment is online and requires an access code. You can obtain a code by purchasing the book *Strengths*

Finder 2.0 wherever you buy books or from the Gallup Strengths Center Store online.[3]

I recently took the test for the first time in ten years so I could share the process with you. It worked like this: I went to the StrengthsFinder website and answered 177 rapid-fire questions that identify pairs of "potential" self-descriptors. (Example: "I dream about the future" versus "People are my greatest ally.") These descriptors anchor opposite ends of a continuum, and you rate yourself on the continuum in one of five places.

You have twenty seconds per question; the short time limit prevents you from overthinking your answers. The questions are supposed to be unfamiliar to you; the idea is that their novelty will better elicit your gut reaction (as opposed to familiar questions evoking the same old answers). If you don't answer a question, the test moves on. That's okay.

Taking the test definitely felt confusing, as though I was making some incorrect choices. But I persevered, knowing this reaction is common.

The whole thing took me about half an hour. When I finished that somewhat nerve-wracking experience, I received my results immediately in my email inbox. That's when the real fun began.

Putting This Information to Work in Your Own Life

The first step in putting the information from the Strengths-Finder assessment to use is to identify your top five areas of greatest potential strength. What are they? How are you currently utilizing them?

I recommend actually taking the assessment, but you could probably get a pretty good idea of your top five strengths by scanning the list of thirty-four themes, paying attention to what resonates, and if you really want to do a thorough job, asking friends and family members what talents they see in you.

With your results in hand, the next step is to get comfortable with your themes.

I Have My Five Themes. Now What?

The assessment told me my top five themes, in order, are:

1. Input
2. Ideation
3. Intellection
4. Strategic
5. Futuristic

Well, well. These themes surprised me. I expected Input and Ideation, but how did Strategic end up on this list? And where was Empathy? I vaguely recalled it being on my list when I took the assessment ages ago. My immediate reaction was to take the test again, but I resisted, remembering that the official literature says your first test gives the "purest and most revealing results."[4] I couldn't recapture the long-lost results from my first test, but I'm pretty sure the StrengthsFinder gurus would have disapproved of me taking the test twice, ten minutes apart, just because I didn't like the results I received.

Thankfully, my answers made more sense as I dug through my results. The nineteen-page Strengths Insight and Action-Planning Guide explained each of my five themes in detail. As I reviewed them, I posed the suggested questions to myself: What words, phrases, or lines stand out to me? Out of all the talents in this insight, what would I like for others to see most in me? One example that answers both questions, from my Futuristic Insight: "Your vision opens people's minds to new and wondrous possibilities."

The Strengths Insight and Action-Planning Guide gives ten "ideas for action" for each of your five themes. To show you what that might look like, here's what I highlighted for my Input theme:

- Schedule time to read books and articles that stimulate you.
- Look for jobs in which you are charged with acquiring new information each day, such as teaching, research, or journalism.
- Partner with someone with dominant Focus or Discipline talents. This person will help you stay on track when your inquisitiveness leads you down intriguing but distracting avenues.[5]

The action points made it easy for me to see how I was already using these themes in my life. From Ideation: "Schedule time to read, because the ideas and experiences of others can become your raw material for new ideas." From Intellection: "Take time to write. Writing might be the best way for you to crystallize and integrate your thoughts." From Input: "Identify situations in which you can share the information you have collected with other people." Me, me, me again.

But the real purpose of the action points was to help me decide what to do next.

Making an Action Plan

The purpose of the StrengthsFinder isn't to *identify* our talents for the fun of it. The point is to develop them into genuine strengths—signature areas where we excel. Raw talent alone doesn't make a strength; instead, our natural abilities are bolstered by the right knowledge and skills. With this end goal in mind, how do we move forward?

The Insight and Action-Planning Guide suggests paying attention to which action items speak to us and highlighting the actions we are most apt to take. For this, I recommend the "Create Action Plan" tool available on the StrengthsFinder website. The tool presents your ten ideas for action for each theme, just like in your guide, with one important difference: each action item contains a check box next to it. I clicked the ones I wanted to prioritize—I chose three or four for each insight—printed my personalized plan, and taped it to my computer monitor.

I appreciated the reminder to focus on building my talents. But I've been here before, as this wasn't my first time going through the process. I've had the opportunity to learn to operate from my strengths, so now let's look at examples of this strategy in action.

The Strengths at Work

My results shone a light on the strengths at work in my own life, of course. It feels good to see a list of all the things you're great at. But the StrengthsFinder also helped me see how I fit into the world around me. My results focused on my five top themes, which means there are twenty-nine others I don't have.

But just because the Achiever theme, for example, isn't prominent for me doesn't mean I don't need this talent in my life. That's where other people come in. I appreciated how my results specifically suggested that I partner with people who have themes different from mine so that, together, we can accomplish things I wouldn't be able to do on my own.

In this sense, the StrengthsFinder affirmed much of what I had already discovered. As a strong Ideation/Intellection/Input person, I need grounded, detail-oriented people to balance me out and help bring my ideas to life. This could mean something as simple as hiring an accountant, photographer, or professional organizer to handle the things in my life that I can't take care of myself.

I found the assessment useful in another way too. I was telling a friend all about my results, and she said, "I hope now you understand why I don't read as much as you do."

"What do you mean?" I asked.

"Well, sometimes I feel like a slacker next to you because you read ten books a month and I read one, if I'm lucky. But your report says reading is a great way to build on your talents. *Your* report. Not mine!"

She had a point.

Bringing People of Different Strengths Together

The StrengthsFinder can help us understand the dynamics at play in our relationships. A friend told me she'd felt increasingly brushed off by one of her neighbors, a local visual artist. My friend was working on a big community project and was deeply involved in the planning stage. Her team had spent a great deal of time reflecting on the nature of community, including its joys and challenges. She was giddy about the project and eager to talk about it. But every time she raised the subject of her work with her neighbor, her neighbor said, "I'm just not interested in that kind of thing."

My friend thought her neighbor was brushing her off because she wasn't interested in *her*. But then my friend took the StrengthsFinder assessment and discovered her top two themes are Intellection and Futuristic. According to her Strengths Insight and Action-Planning Guide, people strong in Intellection "are characterized by their intellectual activity. They are introspective and appreciate intellectual discussions." People strong in Futuristic are "inspired by the future and what could be."[6]

My friend realized her neighbor didn't share her interest in intellectual discussions. She was an artist who lived very much in the here and now, who enjoyed making tangible things with her hands instead of dreaming about ideas. With this insight, my friend was able to appreciate her neighbor for who she was instead of continuing to perceive her disinterest as displeasure.

Let's also look at a simpler example. When a friend found out one of his wife's top themes was Achiever, he realized why it was so important to her to check things off her list every day. She's a stay-at-home mom for now, and he has a demanding job, but they work together to make sure she has time every day to get a few things done. When she's operating out of her strengths, it helps her feel happy and fulfilled in her work.

More of What You Already Are

While I was working on this chapter, a friend came to my home for coffee and spotted *StrengthsFinder 2.0* on my coffee table. "Is that the happy-clappy book that tells everybody how great they are?"

"What, don't you want to find out how great you are?"

She paused. "You know," she said, "I was totally making fun of it just then, but you know what—I do. All I ever hear, and all I ever think about, is what I'm doing *wrong*."

Many frameworks—including the ones in this book—focus on the problems that are plaguing us and how we can escape them. The StrengthsFinder isn't like that. It's focused on making us more of what we already are and on building on what we're doing *right* for a change.

"No pain, no gain" doesn't apply here. Don't feel bad about it. Just enjoy it while it lasts.

Because we're about to confront your junk.

9

Confront Your Junk

the enneagram

I was thirty-one, and I'd decided to go to counseling.

I called the counselor's office—the one provided by my husband's employer—and briefly explained the reason I wanted to see someone. Although, looking back, I can't imagine there was anything "brief" about it. I'm sure I rambled on and on, apologetic and embarrassed, doing my best to explain why I was calling, feeling like an idiot the whole time. It was bad. I told myself that mine surely wasn't the worst phone call she'd had all day. Probably. Hopefully.

The receptionist put me at ease by saying, "I think you should see Patty. She's really good with boundary issues."

I was taken aback. Nowhere in that whole conversation had I used the word *boundary*. I'd never thought of my situation as a boundary issue. What had I said to the receptionist that had made *her* see it as one?

That phone call was the beginning of a long journey. (I feel as though that's a euphemism. Maybe I should throw the word *painful* in there to give you a better idea of what you're in for with this chapter.)

Years later, I understand every bit of that conversation perfectly. I get why the receptionist heard my request and thought *boundaries*. I can clearly see the work I had to do—on myself, I mean—and why. I can see why the receptionist matched me up with Patty (which you and I both know isn't her real name). I can see how I've come a long way and how I still struggle with this stuff occasionally. Okay, regularly, but not as regularly as I used to.

Looking back to that time, I can see I was about to get comfortable with the Enneagram (pronounced *any*-uh-gram), a tool that helps unlock the murky parts of our souls. Like any good personality framework, the Enneagram fosters the self-awareness and self-examination necessary for personal and spiritual growth. It is known for emphasizing each type's negative qualities, which makes it strikingly different from the other frameworks in this book. Exploring our glaring weaknesses and constant stumbling blocks can be a big downer, so please remember as we move forward that this uncomfortable first step flings the doors to positive change wide open.

It took me a long time—a year or maybe more—to become clear on my Enneagram type. I remember the exact moment it clicked for me. But we'll get to that later. For now, let's talk more about the Enneagram's origins.

What You Need to Know about the Enneagram

Like other personality frameworks, the Enneagram serves as a map that helps us better understand ourselves, the people who are important to us, and the groups we're involved in. Its exact origins are murky, but we do know it's been around a long time.

According to Catholic priest Richard Rohr, the roots of the Enneagram's nine types stretch back to a fourth-century Christian monk, Evagrius Ponticus, who listed eight (or nine, depending on the text) vices that impede the way to God. These are anger, pride, vanity, sadness, envy, avarice, gluttony, lust, and laziness.[1] Two hundred years later, Pope Gregory I used these nine vices as a template for the Catholic Church's seven deadly sins. The Enneagram has been used in monasteries for centuries, although it can be and is used by those with different doctrinal beliefs.

While the Enneagram's origins are unclear, we do know that Ivanovich Gurdjieff is responsible for bringing the Enneagram symbol to the modern world, although he didn't go so far as to teach the personality types.[2] Oscar Ichazo and Claudio Naranjo are responsible for the Enneagram of personality types in use today.[3] Helen Palmer, Don Richard Riso, Russ Hudson, Elizabeth Wagele, and Richard Rohr have also contributed to the theory.

The Enneagram is represented by a circle with interior lines connecting the nine types.[4] The nine points on the circle represent nine personality types that interact with the world in their own unique ways. Think of each type as seeing the world through a unique pair of glasses. These glasses sometimes bring us clarity, but they can also distort our vision in big and small ways.

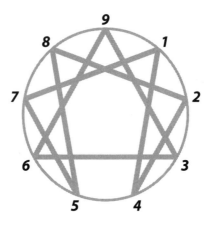

Using the Enneagram, we can look *at* our glasses and understand how they affect the way we see and respond to the world instead of just experiencing the world *through* them without realizing there are other ways to see. The Enneagram can be misused, but when we use it correctly, it can bolster our self-awareness and understanding of the factors at play in our relationships.

Many people say that the Myers-Briggs Type Indicator excels at highlighting our strengths, while the Enneagram unmasks our weaknesses. This isn't exactly true. When I quizzed my friend and Enneagram enthusiast Leigh about this analogy, she corrected me. The Enneagram pinpoints not our weaknesses but our motivations—the underlying reasons that drive everything we do. These motivations can be so much a part of us that we don't even think about them or realize they're driving our behaviors. This is why it's difficult to type someone else on the Enneagram; our type is based not on external traits but on underlying motivations. The external traits are only partial giveaways.

Our motivations are rarely pure. Some practitioners, such as Rohr, even call our persistent driving forces "root sins."[5] The

Enneagram relentlessly focuses on the brokenness of our human motivations, our core struggles, our fatal flaws. It shows how we're inclined to go off the rails in specific, predictable ways.

Discovering our central weaknesses won't make us feel warm and fuzzy. Nor should it. The idea is not to lock us into certain types of behaviors but to pinpoint these behaviors to gain freedom from them. Naming any behavior pattern is the first step in loosening its power. For this reason, the Enneagram has been called a negative system. It's about exposing the bad stuff within us—the things we'd rather not think about or maybe would like to just pretend don't exist.

The Enneagram helps us confront our junk by first showing us what kind of junk we're dealing with. Exposing that hidden stuff we would rather keep covered up is no fun, but it's better to expose it—even though it's painful. Think of it as the diagnosis that comes before the cure.

If you ever hang out with writers, you're sure to hear them say at some point that they hate *writing* but love *having written.* (If you know a writer who claims to enjoy the process, tell them to keep their thoughts to themselves, please.) *Writing* is hard and messy and painful; few writers relish the process. But *having written* is something else entirely. In the same way, *Enneagramming* is brutal. But *having Enneagrammed* feels pretty great. (Those aren't real verbs I just used, but you get my point, right?)

Once we're ready to Enneagram (the verb), the first step is to decide which of the nine types we most identify with.

The Nine Core Types in a Nutshell

Each Enneagram type has its own basic fears, desires, motivations, and core needs. There is nothing wrong with any of these;

the problem is the unhealthy ways we try to dodge our fears, chase our desires, act on our motivations, and fulfill our needs.

It's normal to see a little bit of ourselves in each of the nine types, but according to the Enneagram, we all have one core type that doesn't change. However, each type contains a spectrum of emotional health: a person can be emotionally healthy, average, or unhealthy. These levels fluctuate. We tend to go up and down the levels of health on a day-to-day basis. Some moments we'll be average, some moments we'll be healthy, and some moments we'll dip into the not-so-healthy range. Our current level depends on our self-awareness and progress in our personal growth. Please note that for these purposes, "average" is not "healthy." Pretend you're back in school; "average" doesn't sound so bad, but would you want to bring home a C? Probably not. Most of us have a lot of work to do to achieve emotional health.

The types are called different things depending on the author or resource. The labels I'm using below are from Don Richard Riso and Russ Hudson, founders of the Enneagram Institute and authors of *The Wisdom of the Enneagram*.

Here's a nutshell description of each type:

> One: the Reformer (the need to be perfect).[6] Ones have high standards for themselves and others and a strong sense of right and wrong. Healthy Ones are conscientious and discerning and strive to make things better in appropriate ways. But when Ones go off the rails, they are likely to be critical, resentful, and inflexible and to repress their anger until they explode. Ones naturally seek to gain love by doing things perfectly.

Two: the Helper (the need to be needed). Twos are
caring and helpful, inclined to gain love by
being indispensable. It's easy for women to
mistype themselves as Twos because they're so-
cialized that way; mothers of young children are
especially liable to make this mistake because
helping their children is such a big part of their
lives in this stage. Unhealthy Twos repress their
own needs to tend to the needs of others, but at
their best, Twos delight in appropriately caring
for others and loving them unconditionally.

Three: the Achiever (the need to succeed). Threes are
ambitious, achievement-oriented types who put
their energy into getting things done. They are
competitive and image-conscious. Unhealthy
Threes, driven by a strong need to be recognized, will take these qualities to the extreme.
Healthy Threes can strive to perform well without tying their self-image to the results. Threes
naturally seek to gain love by being successful.

Four: the Individualist (the need to be special). Fours
often focus on what's missing from their lives—
or what they're missing out on—instead of
what they actually have now, in the present.
At their best, Fours are idealistic, empathetic,
and highly creative, but when unhealthy, they
verge into self-pity and despondency and can't
stop longing for what they feel is missing.

Five: the Investigator (the need to perceive). More
than any other type, Fives want to live in their

minds, where they store up knowledge so they can competently face any challenge. They are brilliant analysts and intellectuals, driven to be independent and self-sufficient. At their best, they are perceptive and open-minded visionaries, brilliant trailblazers who seem to notice and understand everything and know what action to take in response. But when unhealthy, they wall themselves off from others entirely, sunk by feelings of inadequacy.

Six: the Loyalist (the need for security). According to Rohr, a full half of the population may be Sixes. Because they are prone to view the world as a dangerously unpredictable place and focus on what could go wrong, these cautious types crave security. At their best, Sixes are responsible, loyal, and trustworthy, but unhealthy Sixes disproportionately perceive the negatives in any situation and doubt themselves excessively.

Seven: the Enthusiast (the need to avoid pain). Sevens are gluttons for the good stuff of life, whether that's interesting ideas or exciting experiences. They want to experience life to its fullest, so they throw themselves into everything they do, which is why this type is sometimes called the Enthusiast. While healthy Sevens do this in a positive fashion, unhealthy Sevens seek these experiences to numb their pain or distract themselves from the unpleasant aspects of life.

Eight: the Challenger (the need to be against). Eights are powerful, dominating types who aren't afraid to assert themselves; they downright fear being weak or powerless because they're under someone else's control. Healthy Eights can be effective crusaders for the causes they believe in, but left unchecked, this same underlying quality can make them aggressive and power-hungry.

Nine: the Peacemaker (the need to avoid). Nines devote their energy to maintaining harmony, both internally and externally. At their best, Nines are true peacemakers, but unhealthy Nines would rather ignore conflict than deal with it. Nines automatically seek to gain love by blending in—substituting others' needs and priorities for their own—instead of trusting they'll be accepted and appreciated for who they are.

This chapter serves as a brief introduction to the Enneagram. If you explore this framework further, you'll learn about the wing types; arrows of integration and disintegration; the head, heart, and gut centers; and much more. Refer to the Recommended Resources for further reading.

A Better Version of Yourself

Growth is a multistep process, but it is an actual *process*. Spiritual formation isn't quite as slippery as some make it out to be. The first step is to crack ourselves open to see what we're hiding, either deliberately or inadvertently, and to drag what is in the dark into the light. This is *the* process of self-discovery and self-awareness.

The goal of the Enneagram is to get the "yuck" out of the way so we can be more ourselves, getting us closer to our true identities and purposes. The Enneagram helps us confront who we really are, what's going on beneath the surface, and what's motivating our behaviors instead of just polishing a shiny, happy facade. It also gives us the tools we need to examine whether change is happening only on a surface level or becoming deeply ingrained in our habits (which would be a good thing). We don't want to change only our behaviors, although we do want those to change. We want lasting change that goes to the heart of who we are. The Enneagram doesn't capture all of who we are; it shows us a mere sliver. It's not the whole truth, but if it can offer us even a glimmer of truth about ourselves, it can empower us to change by first showing us what needs changing and then gently pointing us in the right direction.

While our type doesn't change, the Enneagram helps us work with our personalities to become better versions of ourselves, to attain a greater level of health within our type.[7] The Enneagram helps us imagine what that better self might look like and recognize how we might get there. It also underscores that growing as a person won't in any way "neutralize" our personalities. The goal is, as always, to become *more* ourselves—our true selves—instead of getting tripped up by the stumbling blocks that tend to befall each personality type. Personal growth takes us out of unhealthy reflexive actions and enables us to be more fully ourselves, more present, more aware, and more intentional.

The Enneagram is nuanced and complex, but you need to understand only a few basic concepts to get started. It's more than okay for your knowledge of it to grow while you're using it. You learn by experimenting with the system and with yourself and seeing how your type plays out day by day—both when you're by yourself and when you're interacting with others.

The only requirements are that you have to start where you are and you have to be *ruthlessly* honest with yourself.

Putting This Information to Work in Your Own Life

"Starting" the Enneagram means figuring out your type. Some people are able to nail down their type right away; for others, it's far from a straightforward process. (I belong to the latter group. More on that later.)

There are tests and quizzes, of course, and some are available free online. The highly respected Enneagram Institute publishes a short, free assessment as well as a longer assessment for a fee.[8] My favorite self-test is in *The Essential Enneagram* by David Daniels and Virginia Price, which presents you with short, one-paragraph descriptions containing snapshots of each type. You choose the three you most identify with and take it from there.

These assessments are good starting points, but I recommend determining your type by cozying up with the type profiles. Choose a comfy chair, because this could take a while. As you review the type profiles, pay attention to what resonates. Ask yourself where you best fit. No one description can comprehensively capture your personality, but one type will—as a whole—fit you better than any of the others.

After spending some time thinking it over—and this could mean anywhere from half an hour to a year or more—you'll identify which type suits you best.

Some people, including me, recommend that you wait to dive into the Enneagram until your late twenties or even age thirty because your personality, character, and way of approaching life should be developed before you set out on this journey. This doesn't mean your younger years won't hint at what your type will ultimately become. (For more about the Enneagram and children, especially as it pertains to parenting, I recommend *The Enneagram of Parenting* by Elizabeth Wagele.)

First, You'll Be Miserable

The rule of thumb for Enneagram typing is this: when the yucky stuff resonates, you know you've nailed your type. If you read a description of your Enneagram type and feel exposed, as though you just got caught doing something really embarrassing, that's a sign you typed yourself correctly.

Many years ago, my husband and I hosted his side of the family for a big family get-together. Will and I had just bought a house, and he wanted to give his family—all of whom live out of town—a tour. Everybody piled into cars for a field trip. I stayed behind at the old house to finish the meal prep. (As an introvert, I didn't mind a little alone time, either, as much as I enjoy my husband's family.)

With the house to myself, I cranked up the latest U2 album and got to work heating up dishes, chopping lettuce for salad, filling up glasses with ice. I sang as I worked, because the work goes better that way. At some point, I realized I'd left my water glass in the living room, where we'd been visiting. When I ran in to get it, I discovered my brother-in-law sitting on the sofa, smirking. He'd been there the whole time. Did I mention I am *not* a good singer? I still thank my lucky stars I was wielding sharp knives and fragile glasses that afternoon, or he might have seen me dancing too. This happened fifteen years ago; I think it took me until the ten-year mark to stop turning red when I remembered that moment I realized he'd been there the whole time. And that moment is pretty much what figuring out your Enneagram type feels like. Exposed and embarrassed.

As Richard Rohr is fond of saying, the truth will set you free, but first it will make you miserable.[9] And, whoa, confronting my type certainly made me miserable.

What My Type Identification Process Looked Like

My friend Leigh first piqued my interest in the Enneagram. She sent me some links, recommended a few books, and I rabbit-trailed from there. The first time I read through the Enneagram type profiles I suspected I was a Nine: the peacemaker, healer, reconciler, utopian. But I wasn't certain. This type is motivated by the need to avoid. They fear conflict, aren't great at articulating their wants or needs, and are flexible to a fault. This sounded like me . . . mostly.

Over the months that followed, I returned occasionally to the profiles. I read through the probable suspects again—for me, that meant types One, Five, Seven, and Nine—trying to decide once and for all which type suited me best. I couldn't do it. But I continued to pay attention.

My Enneagram indecision ended the day I had to make a choice that, by its very nature, involved disappointing a lot of people. You're probably imagining a truly epic decision right now, but let me assure you that most people wouldn't have considered it a big deal. Boatloads of people make similar hiring-and-firing-type decisions—the type with clear winners and clear losers—every day. What *was* a big deal was the way I felt absolutely *broken* over the disappointment I was causing. I was sick over it. I kept leaving my house to pace on the little shaded path by my house because I couldn't stop thinking about the people I had disappointed.

I had experienced these emotions before, under similar circumstances. But something was different this time. Thanks to my relatively new knowledge of the Enneagram, I had the self-awareness to realize that while my reaction was pretty extreme, *it was normal for a Nine*. In that instant, I knew my type. For certain. Through the framework of the Enneagram, I could perceive what was driving my behavior: the fear of separation, the yearning for peace of mind, the motivation to avoid conflict at all costs, the need for harmony. *Of course I'm a Nine*, I thought to myself. *Who else reacts like this under this kind of stress?*

This was not a fun realization. It didn't make me feel lovable and unique; it made me feel like a basket case.

But even while I was feeling terrible, I found it enormously helpful to know that because of my type, *I was going to feel terrible in this moment*. The way I was feeling was totally normal—for my Enneagram type. It's how I'm wired. Realizing this made me feel better instantly. Instead of freaking out about why I was feeling drained and borderline depressed, I acknowledged what was going on and why. Conflict makes me crazy. Disappointing people makes me irrational. My reaction was extreme, but I understood that it would fade. I hadn't done anything wrong; these things are just hard for me. My self-awareness freed me to focus on moving forward in a healthy manner (walk, breathe, keep my mouth shut) instead of obsessing about whether I was losing my grip.

The circumstances vary from person to person, but my experience highlights an important point. It's often our glaring weaknesses that confirm our type.

Understanding Your Type

Since I first learned my type, I've had plenty of opportunities to observe it in action, both in my past and in my present. Let's revisit the nutshell description of a Nine.

Nines devote their energy to maintaining harmony, both internally and externally. At their best, Nines are true peacemakers, but unhealthy Nines would rather ignore conflict than deal with it. Nines automatically seek to gain love by blending in—substituting others' needs and priorities for their own—instead of trusting they'll be accepted and appreciated for who they are.

Before I knew my Enneagram type, I knew conflict made me uneasy. I knew *I* could put people at ease. But I was blind to my tendency to blend in, to substitute other people's priorities for my own.

This strikes me as ridiculous now, because examples from my own life are everywhere, and they go way back. Like that time in college I had a friend in my dorm review a paper I'd written for government class on developing nations. He returned my draft covered in notes about how one country in my paper operated like the Death Star and another operated like the Millennium Falcon. He'd given me all the notes I needed to turn my paper into one giant *Star Wars* analogy and convinced me this would elevate my paper from adequate to amazing. Despite my apathy for anything *Star Wars* (minus the Princess Leia Halloween costume I wore when I was eight because *that* was cool), I—and I hate to admit this because it seriously feels worse than getting caught breaking out my Beyoncé moves—incorporated his edits. *I incorporated his edits.* I was a good student who could stand on my own feet, yet I substituted someone else's interests and priorities for my own. Classic Nine. I also got the worst grade of my academic career. (I'm going to go hide in the closet now.)

I could also tell you about when I was a young parent and it was vitally important to me that my friends agreed with the choices I was making about the things new parents get uptight about. Eating and sleeping are the big ones, but I wanted reassurance on everything. I was willing and eager (I'm cringing now, remembering how true this was) to react and adapt to other people's wishes, opinions, and priorities. Classic Nine.

If healthy boundaries have always come easily to you, that's great. It really is. For me, this healthy boundaries thing is possible today only because of a whole lot of hard work and practice. I've gotten much better at it over the years, but it's been a slog. I still need to remain vigilant so I don't forget just where I end and someone else begins.

I don't enjoy recognizing that I behave this way, but doing so makes it possible for me to dial it down. For years, I felt like a nail-biter who'd shellacked her fingernails with one of those foul-tasting polishes that helps her quit biting them because every time she starts to mindlessly chew on her nail, the awful taste screams, "Stop, you're doing it again!" She wears the polish so she can realize when she's lapsing into her bad nail-biting habit.

The Enneagram works similarly to that nasty polish—it helps us fight bad habits. We can learn to put practices in place that will help us realize when we're falling into familiar unhealthy patterns so we can instead learn to choose better ones.

And what does that path of improvement look like? It's unique to each type, but it always begins with awareness.

The Right Questions for Your Type

All of us are inclined to slip up in predictable ways. Because my inclination as a Nine is to be lazy about my boundaries, my goal is to pay particular attention to my propensity to "merge" with others. Over the past few years, I've been able to move the marker a little closer to the "healthy" side of the spectrum by following a process tailored to my type. I've gotten into the habit of noticing when I'm being particularly indecisive (a red flag for me) or when I'm getting sidetracked by other people's priorities and have learned to pause before acting on my (often misguided) impulses. First, I ask myself what *I* want before acting. (Yowzers, did this feel strange at first.) And now I wait before reacting to other people's wishes. I also set my own priorities—on purpose. I screw up a lot, but I at least know what I'm supposed to do.[10]

My behavior may seem crazy to you because these things come easily to you. While I grow by asking myself about my boundaries, you may grow by asking yourself how loud your inner critic has been this week. Or how often you've been feeling disappointed lately about what's missing in your life. Or if you've been escaping the potentially painful stuff by focusing on the new and shiny. These are different questions suited to different Enneagram types; they're designed to probe what's going on beneath the surface for *you*.

These self-care steps aren't exactly easy—for any of us. But I'd rather know what to do for myself—even if it's hard—than not know. Even if it makes me miserable for a little bit.

The Path to Improvement That Is Right for You

How does change actually happen? I've personally found two models to be especially helpful.

I'm a huge fan of the late, great Dallas Willard, whose works have been influential in my personal and spiritual journey. In his wonderful book *Renovation of the Heart*, Willard lays out a model for spiritual growth that he calls the VIM model, named after its three steps: Vision, Intention, Methods.[11] If you're a Willard fan or want an explicitly Christian approach to personal growth and spiritual formation, I highly recommend investigating this model, which lends itself to working in conjunction with the Enneagram (although I can find no evidence that Willard did so himself).

The second model is from David Daniels and Virginia Price's book *The Essential Enneagram*. They call their model the 4As, named after the four things we need to do to make lasting changes in our lives: awareness, acceptance, action, and adherence.[12] Because the 4As were developed specifically to work with the Enneagram, that's the model we'll focus on here.

The 4As Growth Process

Step 1: Awareness

Step 1 on the personal path to wholeness is to figure out what we're dealing with, and the Enneagram excels at delivering this *awareness*. Until we learn to pay attention to our own patterns of behavior, we are powerless to change them.

Many people are afraid this introspective "navel-gazing" is narcissistic or indulgent, but I don't see it that way! It's brutal and necessary work if we truly want to see personal and spiritual growth.

Ironically, learning to see ourselves clearly helps us forget ourselves so we can focus on what matters instead of continually tripping ourselves up. Again, growth of any kind requires us to be honest with ourselves above all. Mindfulness doesn't mean looking for what we want to see; it means watching for what *is*.

Step 2: Acceptance

The next step in the 4As is *acceptance*. If we want to change, we have to be mercilessly honest with ourselves. Acceptance means acknowledging that it is what it is, and we are who we are. This doesn't mean just the bad stuff. True acceptance means seeing the *whole* of ourselves: the good parts and the ugly parts. We're the whole package.

According to Riso and Hudson, before change is possible, we have to believe we're worth the effort to get to know ourselves as we really are.[13] Doing this acceptance step well means showing ourselves compassion as we acknowledge the good and (especially) the bad about ourselves. It means accepting what we find inside ourselves while being gentle and patient with ourselves. (You're not the only person who's going to need compassion, gentleness, and patience for this step.)

This step seems so obvious: yeah, yeah, don't beat yourself up. But remember all those years ago when I went back to counseling? I was *so hard* on myself, week after week. My therapist, Patty, exasperated, finally called me on it and gave me a mental trick that has helped me ever since. I was talking to her about something that happened when I was sixteen, so she asked me if I knew any sixteen-year-old girls. I did. Then she asked me to imagine a sixteen-year-old girl I knew in the same situation I had been in. How did that make me feel? I realized immediately that no sixteen-year-old should have to deal with that crap. My heart went out to my sixteen-year-old self right then. Cultivating compassion for myself isn't always so easy—unfortunately, I still get in plenty of not-great situations, even as an adult—but some variety of that mind trick tends to help.

Acceptance does *not* mean agreeing with or condoning every behavior—whether our own or others'. But when we see what is truly happening, we are empowered to take action to change it.

Step 3: Action

Step 3 is *action*, but the funny thing about the Enneagram growth process is that if I was watching you work through this step, I might not even realize anything was happening.

This step is actually more similar to a sequence. First, to avoid an unhealthy knee-jerk response, we have to pause. Then we have to ask ourselves what's really going on. The goal is to identify what's going on in the moment—what's driving our behavior. In this stage, we're trying to notice our natural reaction and figure out why we're responding that way, whether we're displaying anger, fear, sadness, tears, or whatever. We want to probe beneath the surface, to uncover the thoughts and motivations driving our behavior.

The third step in this action sequence is to move forward consciously instead of out of bad habits or instinctive reactions. Eventually, we want our actions to spring from a healthy place, but that will come with practice, time, and lots of adherence.

Step 4: Adherence

The final step in the 4A growth process is *adherence*, which simply means sticking with it. Adherence means practicing the

4As over and over and over again, until we begin to replace our old, unhealthy habitual responses with more healthy ones. It's similar to building muscle. The more we practice, the easier it gets.

Some people naturally adopt a much more unconscious approach to examining their type or call this process a different thing, such as the spiritual discipline of self-examination. Regardless of what we call it, this is an area in which persistence and discipline will be rewarded.

The process gets easier, but it's never going to be *easy*, and nobody is ever going to do it perfectly. But with time, you'll get better.

Just a Tool, but a Helpful One

The Enneagram is just a tool, yet it remains useful for discovering the mystery of who we are and understanding others around us. As Riso and Hudson point out, "Individuals are understandable only up to a certain point, beyond which they remain mysterious and unpredictable. Thus, while there can be no simple explanations for people as individuals, it is still possible to say something true about them."[14] Paul writes in Ephesians 5:13, "Everything exposed by the light becomes visible—everything that is illuminated becomes a light." It's uncomfortable to dive deep into the darkest parts of ourselves, but it's how we bring those parts into the light.

10

Your Personality Is Not Your Destiny

how much can people change?

When I was a kid, I stumbled through the door of my house one afternoon, distraught. Something had happened at school. Maybe one kid had punched another on the bus or the classmate everyone knew was cheating had finally been caught. I don't remember the inciting incident from that day, but my mother will be pleased to hear that I very much remember what she told me.

As mothers are wont to do, mine gave me encouragement in the form of a warning. "Be careful how you act," she said, "because people don't change that much as they get older."

My mom has lived in the same town most of her life. When she goes to work or church or the grocery store, she's likely to run into adults she babysat when she was twelve or sat behind in math class when she was sixteen. She still gets together with college friends every month. In her experience, most people remain remarkably consistent over the years. The financial advertisements warn us that past performance isn't any indicator of future results, but that student who cheated on a fourth-grade math test isn't someone my mom wants doing her taxes decades later. *And yet.*

A few years ago, I bumped into a woman at the farmers' market I went to high school with. I hadn't seen her in more than ten years. She was with her husband and new baby, enjoying a leisurely weekend away from her bustling pediatrics practice, though she spent a good deal of her time volunteering at the free medical clinic downtown. My high school yearbook wasn't big on handing out superlatives, but I never would have expected that she would have had the discipline to become a pediatrician, or any kind of professional. Or that she would have turned into the sort of person who wakes up before dawn on a Saturday to go to the farmers' market. I couldn't tell you exactly what sort of person that is, but I was sure she wasn't it. In high school, she hadn't been in college-track classes. She was almost kicked out of school after an especially, um, *exciting* spring break trip. And the last time I'd really thought about her was during our junior year, after she spent an evening pretending to be me and prank calling boys. (Thankfully, her cover was blown because one of these boys' homes had a nifty new service called "caller ID.") No one had expected her to go to college, let alone become a pillar of the community.

My mom was right: in many ways, people don't change much over time. But my high school acquaintance's transformation is not an isolated event, either. What's going on here?

In this chapter, we'll explore what about us can't be changed much and what can be changed a lot—and how to make that change happen if we want to.

Personality Change versus Behavioral Change

We've looked at several personality frameworks in this book, which all capture a different aspect of our more-or-less hardwired traits, the ones that are extremely difficult to change even if we want to. Over time, our MBTI and Enneagram types are expected to remain stable. Our love language and our strengths on the StrengthsFinder assessment are too. Highly sensitive children become highly sensitive adults. Over time, these things change a little, but they don't change much. They're part of us, like our height or our shoe size. These are fitting comparisons, because even these things change under the right circumstances, like aging or pregnancy, but they still don't change *much*.

While our personality markers don't change dramatically, they aren't static, either. Research predicts how we'll change over time. With more maturity and life experience, most of us become more conscientious and empathetic—without any conscious effort. Many studies have demonstrated that most adults become more agreeable and emotionally resilient as they age.[1] People also generally become slightly more introverted as they get older. These personality changes are incremental—and gradual.

However, that doesn't mean *we* can't change much; after all, our personalities are only one part of what makes us who we are. Our personalities may be resistant to change, but our behaviors are significantly more pliable. Understanding our personalities makes it significantly easier to change the things within our grasp. This is the whole point of studying the various frameworks! Some people resist personality frameworks because they say such frameworks put them in a box. I've found that understanding my personality helps me step out of the box I'm trapped in. When I understand myself, I can get out of my own way.

The Foundations to Change

How We See Ourselves

"I'm the kind of person who _____" is a powerful phrase, no matter what goes in that blank. Our identities evolve as we move through life. Sometimes this happens without our even noticing. Sometimes we consciously choose to see ourselves in a new way. Consider the new Christian who describes their conversion as taking on *a new identity* in Christ. Or the new mother whose identity profoundly shifts with the birth of her baby.

How do you see yourself? Who are you at your core? Our answers to these questions profoundly change our thoughts and our actions.

Psychologist Scott Barry Kaufman points out that when our identities shift, even our scoring on key personality traits is affected. Not radically, but it *does* impact the scoring. He writes, "As someone becomes more invested in a job, they often become more conscientious; likewise, when someone becomes more invested in a long-term relationship, they tend to become more emotionally stable and have higher self-esteem."[2] If we want to implement successful changes in our lives, how we think about ourselves matters. "I'm the kind of person who _____." What goes in that blank for you?

How We See the World

Our potential to change depends a great deal on whether we believe we *can* change. In other words, if we want to grow and change as individuals, we have to be the kind of people who believe we can. For decades, psychologist Carol Dweck has been studying what she calls "mindset," a simple belief that guides a large part of our lives.[3]

As she sees it, people approach life in one of two ways. Some people believe our characteristics are carved in stone: we have to play the hand we're dealt. These people believe everyone was born with a certain amount of skill, or quality, or intelligence, and these things can't be changed. The die has already been cast; our abilities are static. Dweck calls this a "fixed mindset." If this is you, the cards in your hand determine your destiny.

Others believe that the hand we're dealt is just a starting point. They believe people *can* change over time, improving their natural skills, talents, and abilities through deliberate effort and purposeful engagement. Dweck calls this a "growth mindset." If this is you, your cards are a starting point.

Our mindsets profoundly affect the way we live our lives, and—unlike the frameworks in this book—when it comes to mindset, one option is better than the other. In fact, my friend Paige recently broke up with her boyfriend—who she had once thought was "the one"—because of their differing mindsets. Although Paige had never heard of Carol Dweck, her account of the breakup could have been lifted from the pages of Dweck's excellent book *Mindset*.[4]

If you have a fixed mindset, you see yourself as either smart or not. You're either funny or you're not. You don't see yourself as the kind of person who can change. And when you meet someone and fall in love, that relationship is either good or it's not. You believe that if something doesn't come easily—a job, a skill, a romantic relationship—you should let it go.

Paige's boyfriend had a fixed mindset, while she had a growth mindset and couldn't see a future with a person who didn't believe he could change. (Or perhaps she could envision it just fine and found the idea distasteful.) The research backs Paige up on this. Any relationship expert will admit that a committed long-term relationship is a whole lot of work, and even the best relationships don't come easily. A growth mindset frees us to make an honest assessment and then do something about it.

Marriage expert John Gottman says emotionally intelligent couples understand that the negative stuff is a fact of life in *any* relationship. In fact, he believes most marital arguments aren't solvable, because "most . . . disagreements are rooted in fundamental differences of lifestyle, personality, or values."[5] Gottman believes we grow in our relationships by reconciling our differences, not fixing them. Only a growth mindset makes this possible.

Remember "goodness of fit" in parenting from chapter 5? A fixed mindset says we get what we get. We hope for the best and play the hand we're dealt. But a growth mindset says that goodness of fit isn't something we're assigned; it's something we create. Which mindset would you rather see in your parents, partner, or sibling?

To a large extent, our mindsets determine the quality of our friendships. When we don't feel we need to prove that we're worth something—whether to ourselves or to others—we're free to appreciate other people for who they are. We don't need to belittle them or compete with them to make ourselves feel better. We can encourage one another to grow—in the way that's right for us, and for them.

How We Shape Our Lives

In 1943, Winston Churchill famously said that "we shape our buildings and afterwards our buildings shape us."[6] He was speaking of the British parliamentary Commons Chamber. The shape of the building represented—and thereafter influenced—the shape of the country's government. The same can be said of our lives. We structure our lives how we will; we plot our schedules and fall into rhythm, choose friends and spouses and careers, move into homes, cities, neighborhoods. We shape our lives—and then they shape us.

Gretchen Rubin devoted her book *Better Than Before* to an in-depth study of habits, which she calls "the invisible architecture of everyday life."[7] In the book, Rubin pinpoints four habits as "foundation habits." These are sleep, move, eat and drink right, and unclutter. These four habits disproportionately affect our well-being and directly strengthen our self-control, so changing them makes it much easier to implement *any* change we want to make.[8]

Motivational speaker Jim Rohn made headlines when he asserted that we become like the five people we spend the most time with. We choose our friends and companions, and then they shape us.[9] When we seek out people who are kind, conscientious, and empathetic—which, incidentally, are key predictors of success in life and marriage—we become more kind, conscientious, and empathetic ourselves.

The reverse is also true. This is elegantly observed by Emma Woodhouse in Jane Austen's *Emma*. Mr. Elton is a handsome and ambitious young vicar who is quite charming when he wants to be. After marrying a wealthy but vain woman, Mr. Elton changes—and not for the better. Emma cuttingly observes, "He always was a small man, made smaller by his wife!"[10] The line draws knowing laughs from readers—it's funny because it's true.

In her fascinating book *Rapt*, Winifred Gallagher tells the story of how her cancer diagnosis led to a powerful lesson in mindset. Gallagher decided she could spend the months—and possibly years—of her cancer treatment focusing on the grim diagnosis, or she could purposefully shift her attention to the happier things in her life. She was surprised to discover that when she deliberately focused on the good stuff, she was actually very happy most of the time. She's convinced this was possible only because of her mental vigilance. She writes, "It's about treating your mind as you would a private garden and being as careful as possible about what you introduce and allow to grow there."[11]

We are constantly evolving products of the influences we take into our brains. What we look at, what we long for—to a large extent, this is exactly who we become. The foundational habits we adopt, the people we hang out with, the thoughts we dwell on—these all greatly impact the kinds of people we are and the kinds of people we become, as well as how we change and how much.

Insights that Can Lead to Change

The words of Reinhold Niebuhr's now-famous serenity prayer spring to mind:

> God, grant me the serenity to accept the things I cannot change,
> the courage to change the things I can,
> and the wisdom to know the difference.

I've found that personality insights help me see what changes need to be made, why those changes are necessary, and how to carry them out. Learning more about personality has helped me make peace with the way I was made (even though some days I'd rather trade myself in for a different model). It has helped me understand the people I love, live with, and work with, and it has helped me accept the way *they* were made, which is to say, differently from me.

It's given me the courage to change the things I can (often, the most important thing I'm changing is *my own mind*) while accepting the things I cannot (my immutable personality traits). I'm still learning how to discern the difference, but I do know that thanks to my decade-plus study of personality rubrics, I am now much better at this than I was when I started.

When I first began learning about personality as a teenager, I didn't know how to approach or use this information. I barely had enough self-awareness to determine my type—no matter the framework—let alone put it to work in my life. I might as well have been asking BuzzFeed which Jane Austen leading man I should marry, for all the good it did me.

I've learned a lot since then. I know now that, no matter how much I wish it to be otherwise, parts of me are resistant to change. I'll always be tall, with blue eyes and big feet. Just as surely, I will always be introverted and right-brained, and I'll always need to be a tiny bit more mindful of my personal boundaries than the average woman. I'll struggle with decisions when I get overwhelmed. I'll never love loud music or large crowds. But these things don't define me; they don't determine much of what I can and can't do. My personality traits don't determine my destiny, but they inform it, and I've accepted that.

I've never made a decision based strictly on my personality type. I've never felt that my personality determined my calling. But I've gained a great deal of self-awareness over the years—aided in large part by the personality frameworks in this book—and this self-awareness has empowered me to make better decisions about my life, my relationships, and my work. My personality isn't a limiting label; instead, understanding my personality has blown my possibilities wide open.

Because I understand myself better, I can navigate the world a little better. I've learned how to get out of my own way. My old blind spots don't trip me up nearly as often as they used to. Because I know how I'm likely to go off the rails, it's easier for me to stay on the tracks. This knowledge has vastly improved my self-management and done wonders for my relationships with my friends and family. I don't feel boxed in by my personality; instead, understanding myself has taught me how to open the box and step out of it.

My personality doesn't prescribe my actions, but it does help me thoughtfully consider them in a way I couldn't before. If my personality is the lens through which I see the world, then I've learned to look *at* it instead of just *through* it. I've learned to notice where it's serving me well and where it's stirring up trouble. I've become better at noticing how my lens differs from other people's lenses and what kinds of communication break-downs are likely to result. And then I've learned how to deal with them.

Far from taking away my agency, understanding personality has helped me make smart, informed decisions about my life.

Ready to Climb out of Your Box?

Self-discovery and self-formation are lifelong processes. No one is ever going to have all the answers. We're not going to complete the task of reaching emotional or spiritual maturity, but if we can make substantial progress on the journey, we're doing pretty well.

As I told you in the introduction, I'm not a scholar. I'm a fellow traveler who's found some useful maps and is happy to pass them along to her companions on the road. They can't take you where you need to go—that's still up to you—but they can make the journey much easier. It's not exactly an easy road we're on. I know I'll take all the help I can get.

Truly knowing yourself is one of the hardest things you can do, but it's also one of the most valuable. The sooner you begin, the sooner you'll begin to see the payoff.

Today's a great day to start the journey. If you haven't already, pick a framework—any framework—from this book and dig in. Take the assessment. Make a plan to follow up. Check out one of the resources for further reading at the back of this book. And get ready to climb out of your box.

Acknowledgments

To my editor Rebekah Guzman and the wonderful team at Baker, I'm so fortunate to have landed with you. Thank you for partnering with me to bring these words to life.

To my wonderful agent, Bill Jensen, my deepest gratitude for you and your endless enthusiasm for new ideas. Thank you for partnering with me to bring *this* idea to life.

Liz Heaney, I still can't believe my luck that I got to work with you. This book is inestimably better because of your great eye and sharp hatchet. It was a pleasure.

Catharine Eadens, I owe you big for reading the truly terrible early chapters.

Ed Cyzewski and Christie Purifoy, your first eyes were invaluable.

Seth Haines, I didn't know an INFP could have such a keen eye for structure, which we both know is just what I needed. Thanks for helping me wrangle this book into shape.

Leigh Kramer, this book might be a chapter shorter were it not for your contagious enthusiasm for the Enneagram. I'm grateful for that, as well as for your fact-checking and your friendship, though maybe not in that order.

Erin Odom, you're all the things a due date buddy should be. Thanks for being a sounding board, a cheerleader, and, sometimes, a commiserator.

Kim Vanslambrook, thanks for all the walking and talking, for teaching me there are many ways to read, and for being my MBTI guinea pig.

Myquillyn Smith, Tsh Oxenreider, Emily Freeman, and Emily Lex, thank you for your smarts and savvy and straight talk and kindness.

To the Grown-Ass Ladies: Lisa Patton, Laura Benedict, Joy Jordan-Lake, Marybeth Whalen, and Ariel Lawhon. I'm not sure how I would have pulled this off without you. How is it possible to get so much work done and have so much fun at the same time? *You* are the answer.

And Marybeth and Ariel, thanks for roping me in to your madcap adventures. I learn so much from you and have way too much fun doing it.

To Ginger, Katie, Melissa, and Brenna, thanks for keeping my plates spinning and doing it with style.

To *Modern Mrs. Darcy* readers everywhere, thank you for being the nicest readers on the internet, for your support and enthusiasm, for being the first readers of my fledgling ideas, the whole shebang. I'm so grateful for our community.

To *What Should I Read Next* listeners, it is *so good* to be among people who are reading. Thanks for listening, for inspiring me, and for ensuring I will die with a TBR list thousands of titles longer than I could ever finish.

To my parents, I'm so lucky to have you on my side, from when I was little right up till now. Thank you.

Finally, to Will, Jackson, Sarah, Lucy, and Silas. You are my favorites, forever and ever. On to the next.

Recommended Resources

Introversion/Extroversion

Cain, Susan. *Quiet: The Power of Introverts in a World That Can't Stop Talking*. New York: Broadway Books, 2012.

McHugh, Adam. *Introverts in the Church: Finding Our Place in an Extroverted Culture*. Downers Grove, IL: InterVarsity, 2009.

Highly Sensitive People

Aron, Elaine N. *The Highly Sensitive Child: Helping Our Children Thrive When the World Overwhelms Them*. New York: Harmony, 2012.

———, *The Highly Sensitive Person: How to Thrive When the World Overwhelms You*. New York: Broadway Books, 1996.

———, *The Highly Sensitive Person in Love: Understanding and Managing Relationships When the World Overwhelms You*. New York: Harmony, 1996.

Crawford, Catherine. *The Highly Intuitive Child: A Guide to Understanding and Parenting Unusually Sensitive and Empathic Children*. Alameda, CA: Hunter House, 2008.

Keirsey's Temperaments and the Myers-Briggs Type Indicator

Goldstein, David B., and Otto Kroeger. *Creative You: Using Your Personality Type to Thrive*. New York: Atria, 2013.

Keirsey, David. *Please Understand Me II: Temperament, Character, Intelligence*. Del Mar, CA: Prometheus Nemesis Book Company, 1998.

Myers, Isabel Briggs, with Peter B. Myers. *Gifts Differing: Understanding Personality Type*. Palo Alto, CA: Davies-Black Publishing, 1980.

Quenk, Naomi. *Was That Really Me? How Everyday Stress Brings Out Our Hidden Personality*. Boston: Nicholas Brealey, 2002.

Clifton StrengthsFinder

Gallup Youth Development Specialists. *StrengthsExplorer for Ages 10 to 14*. New York: Gallup, 2007.

Rath, Tom. *StrengthsFinder 2.0*. New York: Gallup, 2007.

Reckmeyer, Mary. *Strengths Based Parenting: Developing Your Child's Innate Talents*. New York: Gallup, 2016.

Enneagram

Baron, Renee, and Elizabeth Wagele. *The Enneagram Made Easy: Discover the 9 Types of People*. San Francisco: HarperSanFrancisco, 1994.

Cron, Ian Morgan, and Suzanne Stabile. *The Road Back to You: An Enneagram Journey to Self-Discovery*. Downers Grove, IL: InterVarsity, 2016.

Daniels, David, and Virginia Price. *The Essential Enneagram: The Definitive Personality Test and Self-Discovery Guide*. New York: HarperOne, 2000.

Palmer, Helen. *The Enneagram in Love and Work: Understanding Your Intimate and Business Relationships*. New York: HarperOne, 1995.

Riso, Don Richard, and Russ Hudson. *The Wisdom of the Enneagram: The Complete Guide to Psychological and Spiritual Growth for the Nine Personality Types*. New York: Bantam, 1999.

Rohr, Richard, and Andreas Ebert. *The Enneagram: A Christian Perspective*. New York: Crossroad Publishing Company, 2001.

Wagele, Elizabeth. *The Enneagram of Parenting: The 9 Types of Children and How to Raise Them Successfully*. New York: HarperOne, 1997.

The Five Love Languages

Chapman, Gary. *The 5 Love Languages: The Secret to Love That Lasts*. Chicago: Northfield Publishing, 1992.

Chapman, Gary, and Paul White. *The 5 Languages of Appreciation in the Workplace: Empowering Organizations by Encouraging People*. Chicago: Northfield Publishing, 2011.

Additional Resources

Dweck, Carol. *Mindset: The New Psychology of Success*. New York: Random House, 2006.

Gallagher, Winifred. *Rapt: Attention and the Focused Life*. New York: Penguin, 2009.

Gawande, Atul. *Being Mortal: Medicine and What Matters in the End*. New York: Metropolitan Books, 2014.

Rubin, Gretchen. *Better Than Before: Mastering the Habits of Our Everyday Lives*. New York: Crown Publishers, 2015.

Willard, Dallas. *Renovation of the Heart: Putting on the Character of Christ*. Colorado Springs: NavPress, 2002.

Notes

Introduction

1. Brent W. Roberts and Wendy F. DelVecchio, "The Rank-Order Consistency of Personality Traits from Childhood to Old Age: A Quantitative Review of Longitudinal Studies," *Psychological Bulletin* 126, no. 1 (January 2000): 3–25.

2. Baffled? It's "sleepy" + "angry."

Chapter 1 My *Aha!* Moment

1. The book is Florence Littauer's *Personality Plus: How to Understand Others by Understanding Yourself* (Grand Rapids: Revell, 1992), which has been reprinted numerous times since its initial printing in 1983.

2. Originally attributed to Miguel de Cervantes, *Don Quixote*, vol. 2, chap. VI. From Spanish "de todos ha de haber en el mundo," which literally translates to "there must be of all [types] in the world." Thomas Shelton, Don Quixote's first translator, wrote this in 1620 as "In the world there must surely be all sorts." It has appeared in various forms since.

3. Henry Southgate, *Many Thoughts of Many Minds: A Treasury of Reference* (London: Griffin, Bohn, and Company, 1862), 338.

4. Christopher Alexander, *The Luminous Ground: The Nature of Order* (Berkeley, CA: Center for Environmental Structure, 2002), 297.

5. David Keirsey, *Please Understand Me II: Temperament, Character, Intelligence* (Del Mar, CA: Prometheus Nemesis Book Company, 1998), 250.

211

Chapter 2 Communication Breakdown

1. Susan Cain, *Quiet: The Power of Introverts in a World That Can't Stop Talking* (New York: Broadway Books, 2012).

2. Maia Szalavitz, "Q&A with Susan Cain on the Power of Introverts," *Time*, January 27, 2012, healthland.time.com/2012/01/27/mind-reading-qa-with-susan-cain-on-the-power-of-introverts/.

3. Isabel Briggs Myers with Peter B. Myers, *Gifts Differing: Understanding Personality Type* (Palo Alto, CA: Davies-Black Publishing, 1980), 7.

4. Scott Barry Kaufman, "Can Personality Be Changed?" *Atlantic*, July 26, 2016, www.theatlantic.com/health/archive/2016/07/can-personality-be-changed/492956/.

5. Cain, *Quiet*, 3; Cain is citing research by Rowan Bayne, Isabel Myers, the Center for Applications of Psychological Type Research Services, and Jean M. Twenge.

6. Szalavitz, "Q&A with Susan Cain."

7. Winifred Gallagher, quoting J. D. Higley, "How We Become What We Are," *Atlantic* 274, no. 3 (September 1994): 48.

8. William Revelle, Michael S. Humphreys, Lisa Simon, and Kirby Gilliland, "The Interactive Effect of Personality, Time of Day, and Caffeine: A Test of the Arousal Model," *Journal of Experimental Psychology: General* 109, no. 1 (March 1980): 1.

9. Ibid.

10. Carl Jung, as quoted by Susan Cain, "The Power of Introverts," TED video, 7:22, filmed February 2012, posted March 2012, www.ted.com/talks/susan_cain_the_power_of_introverts?language=en.

11. Does Jung have the last word on this aspect of personality? Of course not. But it's important to understand his beliefs on introversion and extroversion now or the Myers-Briggs chapters won't make sense later.

12. I like the Quiet Revolution Personality Test found at www.quietrev.com/the-introvert-test, even though it will categorize you as an introvert, extrovert, or ambivert.

13. Adam McHugh, *Introverts in the Church: Finding Our Place in an Extroverted Culture* (Downers Grove, IL: InterVarsity, 2009).

14. Cain, *Quiet*, 19–33.

Chapter 3 Too Hot to Handle

1. Elaine N. Aron, *The Highly Sensitive Person: How to Thrive When the World Overwhelms You* (New York: Broadway Books, 1996), 98.

2. Ibid.

3. Elaine N. Aron, *The Highly Sensitive Child: Helping Our Children Thrive When the World Overwhelms Them* (New York: Broadway Books, 2002), 7–8.

4. Take the self-test for highly sensitive people in *The Highly Sensitive Person*. A similar self-test for highly sensitive children is in her book *The Highly Sensitive Child*. Both self-tests are also available online at hsperson.com/test.

5. Elaine Aron, "Coping Corner: Noise!" *The Highly Sensitive Person Comfort Zone Newsletter* II, issue 1 (February 1997).

Chapter 4 Love and Other Acts of Blindness

1. Gary Chapman, *The 5 Love Languages: The Secret to Love That Lasts* (Chicago: Northfield Publishing, 1992).

2. Ibid., 19–24.

3. Gary Chapman and Paul White, *The 5 Languages of Appreciation in the Workplace: Empowering Organizations by Encouraging People* (Chicago: Northfield Publishing, 2011).

Chapter 5 You're Not Crazy, You're Just Not Me

1. This is a real site, available at www.randombabynames.com.

2. Keirsey, *Please Understand Me II*, 282.

3. Ibid., 22–26.

4. William Shakespeare, *Hamlet*, act 1, scene 2, line 68.

5. Keirsey, *Please Understand Me II*, 4–11; see also www.keirsey.com/sorter /register.aspx.

6. I'm including the corresponding Myers-Briggs shorthand because Keirsey did, and it will ultimately help the reader see how the two systems fit together. If you're unfamiliar with Myers-Briggs and find these notations confusing, don't worry about it now. We unpack that in the next chapter.

7. "Portrait of the Artisan," Keirsey.com, accessed February 28, 2017, www.keirsey.com/4temps/artisan_overview.asp.

8. Keirsey, *Please Understand Me II*, 62.

9. "Portrait of the Guardian," Keirsey.com, accessed February 28, 2017, www.keirsey.com/4temps/guardian_overview.asp.

10. Keirsey, *Please Understand Me II*, 103.

11. Keirsey, *Please Understand Me II*, 100. Keirsey says, "Indeed, nearly half of the forty-one Presidents of the United States have been Guardians, their attitude toward the office summed up in the words of Jimmy Carter: 'The President of the United States is the steward of the nation's destiny.'"

12. L. M. Montgomery, *Anne of Green Gables* (Boston: L. C. Page & Co, 1908), 68.

13. Anne Shirley is, of course, L. M. Montgomery's character from the eponymous novel *Anne of Green Gables* (Boston: L. C. Page & Co, 1908), but this exchange is from the 1985 movie, also called *Anne of Green Gables*, directed by Kevin Sullivan (Toronto, ON: Sullivan Entertainment, 1985).

14. "Portrait of the Idealist," Keirsey.com, accessed February 28, 2017, www.keirsey.com/4temps/idealist_overview.asp.

15. Keirsey, *Please Understand Me II*, 148.

16. *You've Got Mail*, directed by Nora Ephron (Burbank, CA: Warner Bros., 1998), DVD.

17. "Portrait of the Rational," Keirsey.com, accessed February 28, 2017, www.keirsey.com/4temps/rational_overview.asp.

18. Keirsey, *Please Understand Me II*, 195.

19. Jane Austen, *Pride and Prejudice* (London: Thomas Egerton, 1813).

20. Lyle W. Dorsett, ed., *The Essential C. S. Lewis* (New York: Touchstone, 1996), 369.

Chapter 6 Type Talk

1. Myers with Myers, *Gifts Differing*, xi–xv.

2. You'll often see the word *intuition* written as "iNtuition" when MBTI is involved. This is to differentiate the Introversion and Intuition preferences, which both begin with the letter *i*. In MBTI shorthand, I is for Introversion and N is for iNtuition.

3. Charles R. Martin, *Looking at Type: The Fundamentals* (Gainesville, FL: Center for Applications of Psychological Type, 2001).

4. "Estimated Frequencies of the Types in the United States Population," Center for Applications of Psychological Type, accessed March 1, 2017, www.capt.org/mbti-assessment/estimated-frequencies.htm?bhcp=1.

5. Martin, *Looking at Type*.

6. Check out the books in the Recommended Resources section pertaining to the Myers-Briggs Type Index and Keirsey's temperaments. Of the MBTI personality descriptions available online, I especially like those at www.personalitypage.com.

7. Brian Kolodiejchuk, *Mother Teresa: Come Be My Light* (New York: Doubleday, 2007), 34.

8. David B. Goldstein and Otto Kroeger, *Creative You: Using Your Personality Type to Thrive* (New York: Atria, 2013), 131.

9. Ibid., 154.

10. "Quick Facts," CPP, accessed March 1, 2017, www.cpp.com/products /mbti/index.aspx.

11. John M. Gottman, *The Seven Principles for Making Marriage Work: A Practical Guide from the Country's Foremost Relationship Expert* (New York: Harmony, 1999), 129–30.

12. "Take the MBTI® Instrument," The Myers & Briggs Foundation, accessed March 1, 2017, www.myersbriggs.org/my-mbti-personality-type /take-the-mbti-instrument/.

13. The official MBTI assessment is exclusively administered by CPP and can be taken at www.mbtionline.com/TaketheMBTI. The cost at time of publication was $49.95, plus tax.

14. Found at www.16personalities.com/free-personality-test.

15. Go to www.personalitypage.com/html/portraits.html to access Personality Page Type Portraits for each of the sixteen types.

16. Goldstein and Kroeger, *Creative You*, 131.

Chapter 8 Play to Your Strengths

1. Tom Rath, *StrengthsFinder 2.0* (New York: Gallup, 2007), i.

2. Ibid., 20.

3. The Gallup Strengths Center Store can be found at www.gallupstrengths center.com/purchase/en-US/Product?Path=Clifton%20StrengthsFinder. The cost at time of publication was $15.00.

4. "Frequently Asked Questions," Gallup Strengths Center, accessed March 2, 2017, strengths.gallup.com/help/general/125483/retake-Clifton-Strengths Finder-assessment-taking-Clifton-StrengthsFinder-once-af-aspx.

5. These ideas for action were included in my personalized Strengths Insight and Action-Planning Guide; however, ideas for action for all thirty-four themes can be found in *StrengthsFinder 2.0*.

6. Ibid.

Chapter 9 Confront Your Junk

1. Richard Rohr and Andreas Ebert, *The Enneagram: A Christian Perspective* (New York: Crossroad Publishing Company, 2001), 8–11.

2. Don Richard Riso and Russ Hudson, *The Wisdom of the Enneagram*, (New York: Bantam, 1999), 22.

3. Ibid., 22–25.

4. The name *Enneagram* comes from the Greek words *ennea*, meaning nine, and *gram*, meaning something written or drawn.

5. Rohr and Ebert, *The Enneagram*, 33.

6. Ibid., xii–xiii; type descriptions for the nine types given here (e.g., "the need to be perfect").

7. Riso and Hudson, *The Wisdom of the Enneagram*, 75.

8. Available at the Enneagram Institute's website: www.enneagraminstitute .com.

9. Richard Rohr, *Everything Belongs: The Gift of Contemplative Prayer* (New York: Crossroad Publishing Company, 1999), 75.

10. I like the reflection questions for each type in David Daniels and Virginia Price's book *The Essential Enneagram: The Definitive Personality Test and Self-Discovery Guide* (New York: HarperOne, 2000).

11. The VIM method in a nutshell:

Vision: First, you need to catch the vision of where you could go, of who you could be if you changed. What would that person look like? Picture it in your mind's eye.

Intention: Commit to the process. Willard calls this our "intention." You must decide that you truly intend to change and are willing to do what it takes to make that happen. In theory, this is the simplest step, although getting to the point where you're ready to change is anything but easy. For effective change to happen, you have to decide to do it.

Methods: Finally, you must determine methods, or practices, that will make this change possible. For Willard, this often meant the classic spiritual disciplines: reading, prayer, reflection, worship, solitude.

12. Daniels and Price, *The Essential Enneagram*, 80–109; these pages contain an in-depth examination of what the 4As look like for each Enneagram type.

13. Riso and Hudson, *The Wisdom of the Enneagram*, 35.

14. Don Richard Riso and Russ Hudson, *Discovering Your Personality Type: The Essential Introduction to the Enneagram* (New York: Houghton Mifflin Company, 2003), 87.

Chapter 10 Your Personality Is Not Your Destiny

1. Christopher J. Soto, Oliver P. John, Samuel D. Gosling, and Jeff Potter, "Age Differences in Personality Traits from 10 to 65. Big Five Domains and Facets in a Large Cross-Sectional Sample," *Journal of Personality and Social Psychology* 100, no. 2 (February 2011): 330–48.

2. Kaufman, "Can Personality Be Changed?"

3. Carol S. Dweck, *Mindset: The New Psychology of Success* (New York: Ballantine, 2006).

4. Ibid.

5. Gottman, *The Seven Principles for Making Marriage Work*, 23.

6. Winston Churchill, speech in the British House of Commons regarding the rebuilding of the Commons Chamber, which was destroyed by German bombs during the blitz, October 28, 1944. London, October 28, 1943.

7. Gretchen Rubin, *Better Than Before: Mastering the Habits of Our Everyday Lives* (New York: Crown Publishers, 2015), xi.

8. Ibid., 58–73.

9. Aimee Groth, "You're the Average of the Five People You Spend the Most Time With," Business Insider, July 24, 2012, www.businessinsider.co m/jim-rohn-youre-the-average-of-the-five-people-you-spend-the-most-time -with-2012-7.

10. Jane Austen, *Emma* (London, 1815).

11. Winifred Gallagher, *Rapt: Attention and the Focused Life* (New York: Penguin, 2009), 53.

When it comes to approaching her writing and life, **Anne Bogel** takes a line from Emily Dickinson: "I dwell in possibility." She is adept at viewing old ideas from a fresh perspective and presenting them to the reader in such a way that they experience them as if for the first time.

In 2011, Anne launched *Modern Mrs. Darcy*. Her blog, which derives its name from Jane Austen, didn't slot neatly into the existing blog niches (although she's been pleased to hear it described back to her as "a lifestyle blog for nerds"), yet it quickly gained a cult following of smart, thoughtful readers who loved Anne's modus operandi of approaching old and familiar ideas from new and fresh angles.

Anne blogs frequently about books and reading on her site. Her book lists are among her most popular posts. She is well-known by readers, authors, and publishers as a tastemaker. In 2016, she launched her podcast *What Should I Read Next*, a popular show devoted to literary matchmaking, bibliotherapy, and all things books and reading.

Anne lives in Louisville, Kentucky, with her husband and four children.

Hi! I'm Anne

Connect with my blog, book club, and podcast *(What Should I Read Next?)* at **ModernMrsDarcy.com** and **AnneBogel.com**.

WHAT SHOULD I READ NEXT?

with anne bogel

⊙ AnneBogel   🐦 AnneBogel   f ModernMrsDarcy

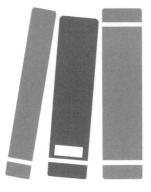

LIKE THIS
BOOK?
Consider sharing it with others!

- Share or mention the book on your social media platforms. Use the hashtag **#ReadingPeople**.

- Write a book review on your blog or on a retailer site.

- Pick up a copy for friends, family, or anyone who you think would enjoy and be challenged by its message.

- Share this message on **INSTAGRAM** and **TWITTER**: "I loved #ReadingPeople by @AnneBogel"

- Share this message on **FACEBOOK**: "I loved #ReadingPeople by @ModernMrsDarcy"

- Recommend this book for your book club, workplace, class, or church.

- Follow Baker Books on social media and tell us what you like.

 Facebook.com/ReadBakerBooks

@ReadBakerBooks